KIDZ THAT DREAM BIG!...

*Essential Tips on How to Have **FUN**, **DREAM BIG** and Make Money Doing What You **LOVE***

LASHAI BEN SALMI
&
TRAY-SÉAN BEN SALMI

Published by New Generation Publishing in 2012

Copyright © Lashai Ben Salmi & Tray-Séan Ben Salmi 2012

First Edition

The author asserts the moral right under the Copyright, Designs and Patents Act 1988 to be identified as the author of this work.

All Rights reserved. No part of this publication may be reproduced, stored in a retrieval system or transmitted, in any form or by any means without the prior consent of the author, nor be otherwise circulated in any form of binding or cover other than that which it is published and without a similar condition being imposed on the subsequent purchaser.

www.newgeneration-publishing.com

 New Generation **Publishing**

'YOU' called this book to you because you live in an insane world and you want to change it. Well that's all going to change... Right here, right now with this book, because we are going to teach you how to Have **FUN**, **DREAM BIG** & Make money doing what you **LOVE** now! Everything starts with an idea or concept in your mind. The idea or concept is given form by taking action and manifesting your **dream**s. Then the magic begins to happen during the construction process. That process begins here and **now** (((**SMILE**)))! Are you ready? Yes or Yes?

This book is dedicated to children and youth everywhere...

This book is not intended to provide personalised legal, financial or investment advice. The Authors and the Publisher specifically disclaim any liability, loss or rick which is incurred as a consequence, directly or indirectly, of the use and application of any content of this work.

We have every confidence that this book can assist you to have **FUN, DREAM BIG**, make money doing what you **LOVE** and so much more.

Editing by: Miss Lashai Ben Salmi, Tray-Séan Ben Salmi, Mrs Sabrina Ben Salmi BSc & Ms Mary Paul

Cover Design by: Ricky Maye
E: ricky@rickymaye.com W: www.rickymaye.com

ACKNOWLEDGEMENTS

We **LOVE** OUR LIFE (((**SMILE**))) - We thank **God** for our abundance of wealth, health, opportunities, support and happiness. We appreciate our mother, stepfather and grandmother, Yasmine (junior sister) and Mohamed-Salah (junior brother)**.** We also appreciate the support of: Dawn Gibbins MBE. Froggo Marketing: Mark Donnan, Toby Street & James Downton. Robert G. Allen & Angii Anderton. Debbie Stoute. Ramasamy Kavitha. Melanie Stewart. Junior Ogunyemi. Alex Browning. Auntie Nahid, Alena & family. Stephanie J Hale. Pauline Maxwell. Gesmay Paynter. Ray Lewis. Mark Sheahan. The Exchange Ilford: Jayne Burton. Lime Tree: Malcolm Graham & Amelia Humfress. A.S.A.E: Andrew Sage. Art Against Knives: Katy Dawe & team. Elaine Summers & Jade. Majid Khan. White Out Originals: Mahmood Shaikh & Team. Brown Rudnick: Georgie Collins & Team. Andy Harrington. Vishal Sharma & Family. ClearlySo: Rodney Schwartz, Simon Evil, Phillipa Jackson & Team. Live Unltd, Young Citizen Award, Black Youth Achievements Award, TEDx Salford: Mishal Saeed. Blak Pearl: Vishal Mishal. Mind Protein: Ralph Plumb & team. Raymond Aaron & team. Ultimate Blueprint Event: Jeff Vacek & Ken Preuss. Julie Holness of Fearlessly Speaking. Stedman Graham. WTF: Marco Kozlowski. Mayfield Secondary School and Loxford Secondary School. Everyone at New Generation Publishing. Also to all our interviewees and everyone who helped us.

We would also like to take this opportunity to acknowledge those of you who delivered adversity to our lives because this made us stronger and inspired us to convert our adversities into empowerment. After all we are who we are today as a direct result of everything we experienced *(((SMILE)))*.

We would like to thank those who we do not know personally yet, but inspired us Oprah Winfrey, Neale Donald Walsch, T Harv Eker, Richard Branson and Robert T. Kiyosaki

CONTENTS

FOREWORD 6
A MESSAGE FROM US TO YOU 10
MY JOURNEY & OUR JOURNEY 13
HOW DOES THIS RELATE TO YOU? 24
BE THE BEST YOU CAN BE 28
BEING YOU IS A PIECE OF CAKE POEM 30
SHOW RESPECT FOR YOUR LIFE AND OTHERS 31
SOLACE 32
OBEY YOUR PARENT(S)/GAURDIAN(S) 35
MUSIC 37
LEARN TO **LOVE** 'YOU' 38
IMPROVE RELATIONSHIPS NOW (((**SMILE**))) 39
YOU CAN CHANGE YOUR LIFE 42
THE MONEY GAME 52
EMOTIONS 54
I **LOVE** MY LIFE 59
YOU ARE UNIQUE 60
HARMONIOUS 62
YOU ARE THE MASTER OF YOUR MIND! 64
CONVERT YOUR ADVERSITY INTO EMPOWERMENT. 67
ISSUES FACED BY CHILDREN AND YOUTH 69
IT IS SIMPLY A MATTER OF CHOICE 71
YOU HARNESS AN AMAZING ABILITY 72
CHOOSE TO BE HAPPY 76
ASK - BELIEVE - RECEIVE 79
FORGIVE AND LET GO 83
BULLYING 88
PLANT YOUR SEED FOR FINANCIAL EDUCATION . 90
DREAMS DO COME TRUE 113
WE BELIEVE IN YOU! 114
MAKE MONEY DOING WHAT YOU **LOVE** 115
WHAT THE EXPERTS SAY 118
CONNECTING THE DOTS & GETTING STARTED ... 124
ABOUT THE AUTHORS 129

Imagine how you'll feel as you finish reading the last page of this book...... (((**SMILE**)))

Foreword

What do you want most? Is it money, love, health, wealth, happiness, fame, power, contentment, peace of mind?

The contents of this book contains what the title says... and what an awesome title might I add "Kidz that DREAM BIG – Essential tips on how to have FUN, DREAM BIG and make money doing what you LOVE."

The essential tips described in this book offer children and youth a valuable insight to a dependable philosophy of how to have FUN, DREAM BIG and make money doing what you LOVE. This book is not only for your benefit, but for each and every person you connect with in your journey. If you're searching for a definite goal in life I highly recommend this book to all children, youth and individuals alike – who want to have FUN, DREAM BIG and make money doing what they LOVE. Before beginning the book you will benefit hugely if you recognize the fact that the book was written by two inspirational authors Lashai Ben Salmi (11) and Tray-Séan Ben Salmi (7) and the contents has a wealth of benefits inside. If you are willing to take action allow Lashai and Tray-Séan to teach you how to convert your adversities into empowerment.

I mean it when I say that you cannot digest the contents of this book properly in a few days, a week or a month. After reading the book thoroughly it is evident that this textbook contains valuable essential tips on how to have FUN, DREAM BIG and make money doing what you LOVE. I urge children and youth to study this book - this book should be digested. Underline the sentences which impress, inspire and motivate you most. Later, you should go back to these marked lines and read them again.

Do not merely read this book, absorb its entire contents and make them your own. This book should be adopted by all school, charities, community and government bodies and all children and youth support groups across the globe - no child or youth should be without a copy of this book. This book will help you to organize and apply the knowledge acquired and inspire you to convert your adversities into empowerment. The authors have done very well at conveying their personal journey, knowledge and experiences of exchanging their adversities into empowerment and more importantly having a dream then manifesting it!

What I most like about this book is that it is touchable for children and youth across the globe, no matter what their circumstances may or may not be. Lashai is only 11 and Tray-Séan only 7 they found a problem, came up with a solution and packaged their ideas. They have turned their love for people into several business ideas. I first meet Lashai in 2011 when she attended my event: Multiple Streams of Millions and Lashai interviewed me and Mark Donnan to upload on to her website and I was extremely impressed with her interview questions. I then invited Lashai to take the stage and speak to my entire audience about her experience of bullying; might I add that Lashai also recorded an excellent video testimony for my event. I feel that this is merely the beginning of this amazing Ben Salmi Duo so watch this space.

The Ben Salmi Duo co-created their first App called: Put the RED CARD up to bullying in short Red

Card It! They also have an online store: www.zazzle.com/redcardit this demonstrates not only did they avoid adopting a victim mentality they actively created a victorious one within their life journey using the techniques contained in this book. The Ben Salmi Duo are on a mission to share their knowledge and experience with children and youth across the globe in the hope of inspiring you to rise up empowered and to remind you that you to can achieve the same or better.

After reading this book you will realize that you have come into possession of a philosophy which can be transmuted into material wealth or serve as readily to bring you peace of mind, understanding spiritual harmony and in some instances as in the case of the authors, it can help you master physical affliction.

The authors have been taught to analyze, mirror and match successful people, and adapt the habit of exchanging ideas through what is commonly called conferences. When the Ben Salmi Duo encounter challenges to be solved they sit down together as a family to discuss the matters at hand, ask friends and talk freely until they discover solutions and a plan that would serve the purpose at hand from joint contribution of ideas from all in question.

You who read this book will get most out of it by putting into practice the master mind principle. This you can do by forming a study group consisting of any desired number of people who are friendly and harmonious together. The group should have a regular meeting as often as possible for example once a week. The procedure should consist of reading one chapter of the book at each meeting, and then the contents of the chapter should be freely discussed by all members. Each member should make notes, putting down all ideas of his/her own inspired by the discussion. Each member should carefully read and analyze each chapter several days prior to the meeting. The reading at the club should be done by someone who reads well and understands how to put colour and feeing into the lines being read. If you commit to taking action you will be almost certain to gain positive learnings and go on to have FUN, DREAM BIG and make money doing what you LOVE or better - after all you are a creator...

Just Do IT!

Robert G. Allen

Mentor, Speaker & International Bestselling Author *Creating Wealth*, *Multiple Streams of Income*, *Multiple Streams of Internet Income*, *Nothing Down*, *Nothing Down for Women*, *One Minute Millionaire*, *Cracking the Millionaire Code*, and *Cash In A Flash*.

A MESSAGE FROM US TO YOU

Hi there! It's Lashai and Tray-Séan Ben Salmi also known as the Ben Salmi Duo (((**SMILE**))). Welcome to the family and your **New Life** - a life of having **FUN, DREAMING BIG** and making money doing what you **LOVE**.

Through us children and youth - just like you, are inspired to convert their adversity into empowerment.

We are here to awaken you from your fantasy by reminding you of the unbounded potential surrounding you right **now**. We are the eldest of four siblings Lol! Lol! Lol! The pressures of being that... We are here to simplify the process by sharing our knowledge, experiences and so much more with you.

We are passionate about community cohesion that is why we co-authored this book and co-created our first App called: Put the RED CARD Up To Bullying nicknamed "RED CARD IT!" our app aims to reduce bullying and increase community cohesion – check it out... We also have an online store via: www.zazzle.com/redcardit

We are your friend, ones you can trust. We are determined to change the lives of children and youth across the globe for generations to come. We are the Ben Salmi Duo and our mission is to remind you of your hidden potential.

Is our task scary? Yes! From time to time, but we will not stop! We are the Ben Salmi Duo and we will not allow our fear to stop us. We have chosen to make our passion greater than our fear. We believe that following others is what got so many children and youth into confusion.

Hay lets face it... it's going to take action, focus, unwavering faith and words to awaken the hearts and minds of children and youth who have un**know**ingly been lead astray.

We have lived through the disappointment, friendship issues, parental disagreements, sibling disagreements, parental separation, stereotypes, isolation, bullying, confusion, boredom etc, etc, etc. So what! What matters most, is what you choose to do right here and right now. We chose to convert our adversities into empowerment and preserve the positive learnings for ourselves, you and for the future.

We are the Ben Salmi Duo and we don't believe that hope alone gets anyone anywhere. Why hope when you can **TAKE ACTION**, have **FUN**, **DREAM BIG** and make money doing what you **LOVE**. We believe that it is vital to maintain the (((**FUN FACTOR**)))... That's what good teachers do - right? Yes or Yes? We **know** some children and youth simply will not **STEP UP now**. They are simply too lazy, too comfortable or simply too scared and wasting time in the fantasy of false security and so called enjoyment to take control of their lives.

Nevertheless we do k**now** that some will come around. When they do, we'll have resources for you: Apps you can download. Books you can read. FREE STUFF you can (((**SMILE**))) about and Workshops you can attend to name a few...

We have many doors and every one of them is open to the **willing** no matter what your circumstances. Remember creating a bright future all starts with a **dream** and then a will to **TAKE ACTION** today. In order to become successful tomorrow you must simply plant a seed today. We recognize that creating a bright future means expanding beyond your current understanding, remember we are the Ben Salmi Duo and we are your friends. **N**ow time to have **FUN**,

DREAM BIG and make money doing what you **LOVE**. We all have **dream**s... right? Yes or Yes?

Are you ready to embrace the abundance of life? Yes or Yes?

NOW! Take a deep breath, and then take a moment to preserve the positive learnings for yourself and for the future...

This book is our gift to you; it contains really useful tips that can help you to have **FUN**, **DREAM BIG** and make money doing what you **LOVE** and so much more if you are willing...

Let's face it, like any gift you'll only enjoy the benefits when you use it. Here's to your journey of having **FUN**, **DREAMING BIG** and making money doing what you **LOVE**.

Oceans of **LOVE**, positivity and best wishes from your friends Lashai & Tray-Séan Ben Salmi

Xxx *(((SMILE)))* xxX

MY JOURNEY & OUR JOURNEY

Lol! We know! We know! The title may appear odd but, for those of you who might not already know *MY JOURNEY "Giving youth several reasons to (((SMILE)))" & OUR JOURNEY "Giving children several reasons to (((SMILE)))"* are the names of mine and my brothers' projects.

We can still remember when we discovered that we could have **FUN**, **DREAM BIG** and make money doing what we **LOVE**. It all began during our 6 weeks summer holiday break 2011. I was nominated for two awards; Live Unltd & Young Citizen Award. A few weeks later I had to attend a Live Unltd interview and felt absolutely sick at the thought of it. Lol! – Everything was fine when exchanging emails and during telephone calls, yet the thought of the interview made me feel sick. This was my first ever interview, so it made me feel scared because I didn't know what to expect. Mum and I arrived at the Unltd office 15 minutes early. As the development manager introduced herself I felt as if I didn't even know my own name... Lol! Whenever I tell this story we always laugh. During the interview I was overwhelmed with mixed emotions because I also felt excited about explaining my project proposal and what I'm passionate about:

➢ I'm passionate about designing clothing

➢ I'm passionate about inspiring & motivating children and youth

➢ I'm passionate about reducing bullying, increase community cohesion and assist bullies/victims of bullying to have fun, dream big and make money doing what they love an so much more

➢   I'm passionate about science.......... and so on

FYI Live Unltd grants are for individuals who have ideas which could benefit themselves and their community.

FYI I was soooo… worried that my idea would not be good enough, and that they may not like me and that they wouldn't take me seriously because of my age (I was 11 at the time).... The interview was tough especially when she asked me to reduce my initial budget proposal from £5,000 to £500 (because there was an error on their website as they only grant a maximum of £500 to 11 year olds). Ouch!... I was given a deadline for the following morning... at that precise moment my heart skipped a beat – (((I felt like fainting Lol!))).

However I remained focused and passionate about my **dream** and asked my yummy mummy to assist with adjusting my budget and emailed it to the development manager as requested.

At that point I didn't feel confident at all – because I still needed £5,000 to create and launch the App. OGM! OGM! OGM! Where on earth would we get the remaining £4,500 from? What if my Live Unltd application isn't successful?...

Several weeks passed by, Tray-Séan and I kept talking about our dreams and aspirations to maintain focused upon our WHY? We created **dream** boards, business focus collage folders and then our yummy mummy nominated us both for an award called the Young Citizen Awards. Only one of us made it through to the final stages... we are a team so it was a huge achievement for at least one of us to get through to the final stages.

Hooray! Hooray! Hooray!

Weeks later there was a letter addressed to (((ME))) it read: Miss Lashai Ben Salmi, as I was only 11 years old and didn't usually get mail - sooooo it was very exciting (((**SMILE**))) to say the least.

It read something like this:

"Dear Lashai, CONGRATULATIONS you have been awarded a Live Unltd Award"

Hooray! Hooray! Hooray! We all began to dance... Hooray! Hooray! Hooray! OMG! OMG! OGM! The feelings that I felt cannot be put into words. This was the first time I received mail, let alone (((**WIN**))) anything.

My list of aspirations:

- My Journey "Giving youth several reasons to (((SMILE)))"
- App "Red Card It"
- Book "Kidz that **DREAM BIG**"
- Fashion label "Fashion Lash-Lash"
- Short story competitions "Mega Lash-Lash Competitions"

Tray-Séan's list of aspirations:

- Our Journey "Giving children several reasons to (((SMILE)))"
- App "Red Card it"
- Book "Kidz that **DREAM BIG**"
- Fashion label "Fashion Shuby"
- Short story competitions "Mega Shuby Competitions"

Our hearts were beating rapidly and our minds were heavily populated with flashbacks of prior adversities. In our hearts we knew that we were going to exchange our adversities for empowerment and in doing so we were going to inspire children and youth to rise up empowered *(((SMILE)))*. We still did not know how, but we could feel with all our hearts that we would.

That week we picked up our local news paper and we spotted my photo, it seemed as if it was a repeat submission! I felt a little sad and simply expressed absolute gratitude for winning one out of the two awards then we went home. When we were showing our grandmother the news paper and explaining that I did not win, our grandmother said stop playing games LOL! You won - to our surprise it wasn't a repeat submission... Yippee! Yippee! Yippee! We realised that I had in fact won... Hooray! Hooray! Hooray! This is the second award in one MONTH - OGM! How amazing. Tray-Séan and I shouted out "**Dreams** do come true" then we began to dance and sing and celebrated as a family.

We preserved the positive learnings for our selves, you and for the future. We **now know** that all of our prior adversities were solely to prepare us for that very moment. We were overwhelmed with gratitude *(((SMILE)))*. Our yummy mummy contacted Ilford Recorder and the Voice newspaper, and shortly after an article was published announcing my awards in the hope of inspiring others. Following that Tray-Séan and I were also interviewed by Raising CEO Kids and then I was interviewed by Your Hidden Potential. The Ben Salmi Duo continued to attend events; I was invited to attend the ClearlySo Social Business Conference and pitched our App idea. It was a truly unforgettable experience because I was also interviewed by Lewis

Johnson (brother of the Mayor of London Boris Johnson).

What ClearlySo said about me:

- Tom Cropper, posted on 13.10.11:

- "There were some memorable presentations: 12 year old Lashai Ben Salmi broke new ground by becoming the youngest entrepreneur to pitch at any ClearlySo event when she presented her anti bullying app."

- "Flying pants, the youngest social entrepreneur in the UK"

- "We saw it also in the Social Business of the Year Award in which 12 year old Lashai Ben Salmi brilliantly pitched her anti bullying app to the entire audience. This is an experience which reduces many seasoned entrepreneurs into gibbering wrecks, but she took it on with aplomb. We first ran into her at one of our teatimes, and she's been tearing up the sector ever since."

Rod Schwartz, posted on 07.11.11

- "When Lashai Ben-Salmi rose to pitch her business, My Journey, she held the audience in rapt attention as she told them about her phone app designed to help combat bullying in schools. For experienced entrepreneurs 45 seconds can be daunting, but she appeared calm and competent in getting the main points of her story across."

I attended a Robert G Allen (with our mum and auntie Gesmay Paynter) event and was invite by Robert G Allen to speak to the entire audience about my experience of being bullied and networked like crazy FYI I was scared, but did it anyway. I am glad I did because it resulted in securing investment towards our first App (from Dawn Gibbins MBE). Froggo Marketing also sponsored us to create the My Journey new logo and website and as you know Robert G. Allen wrote our book foreword. We continue to be friends with them all. Dawn Gibbins MBE helped us to find someone to work on our App - Andrew Sage of Andrew Sage Art and Entertainment teamed up with Graham Malcolm and Amelia Humfress of Lime Tree to create our very first app. A couple of months later I was nominated for a Black Youth Achievements Award and ((((**WON**)))) in the category of technology. Yes, we experienced a lot of challenges along the way... but from that moment things just got better and better and we just continued to build relationships and attended TEDx Salford in support of our friend Dawn Gibbins MBE who was amazing on stage (((**SMILE**))). We went to dinner with new friends Mr & Mrs Ashworth, Christine McGrory, the event organisers and all of the event speakers which was ((((**AWESOME**))))) because there was a NASA astronaut called Ron Garan how crazy is that... we **LOVE** our life *(((SMILE)))*. We continued to read books like: Who Moved My Cheese?, Become a KEY PERSON of INFLUENCE, Conversations with God – for teens, Rich Dad, Poor Dad too name a few... Lol! We didn't complete them all but were still inspired

(Mum bottom left, Tray-Séan in the middle, me on the bottom right, Dawn holing me and Christine above in the middle)

Tray-Séan and I learned that:

Movement in a new direction helped us to create new and wonderful result - beyond our wildest **dreams.**

My head teacher at Mayfield Secondary School wrote a letter to our mother and stepfather commending them and me for all of my achievements. At that precise moment in our life we knew that we were taking steps towards manifesting our **dreams**. Just like our yummy mummy and yummy grandmother we have always enjoyed helping others. We always share our knowledge with children and youth and everyone who knows us, friends, family and at times total strangers. Tray-Séan and I decided to co-author this book to share our positive learnings with you.

FYI when we spoke to people about our ideas; we didn't always get positive feedback from - time to time people didn't take us seriously because we were children. Well that was until they saw our visual business plan, watched our YouTube channel, received our business cards, navigated our websites and researched our online profiles. When we have bad days we simply spoke to our yummy mummy, yummy grandmother, friends etc about our feelings, listened to our hearts and continued to watch movies such as: What the bleep do you know, Thrive, Instinct and The Secret etc. Before we knew it we successfully attracted the remaining pieces to our puzzle and our App became a reality. We remain hungry to learn because we are having **FUN**, **DREAMING BIG** and learning how to make money doing what we **LOVE**. Words can't explain how amazing we feel. Everyone experiences challenges so you just have to stay focused, because challenges do not define who you are; you choose how to react to adversities. Besides, adversities are merely extreme forms of market research LOL!... My Journey & Our Journey experienced a lot of challenges but it was all worth it in the end. The experiences helped us to grow beyond our wildest **dream**s. Living our life with passion and purpose has gifted us unique opportunities, freedom, priceless experiences, k**now**ledge, amazing and exclusive network of support, inspiration, confidence and so much more. The **big**gest gain and more importantly we have and continue to positively impact the lives of children, youth and even adults from a range of financial backgrounds.

This feeling is enormously fulfilling because we k**now** that by having **FUN**, **DREAMING BIG** and making money doing what we **LOVE** inspires you to do the same or better. We are enjoying our dance with the universe *(((SMILE)))*.

At the time of writing our **dream**s down on paper we didn't k**now** *'how'* we'd achieve them, but we had a huge *'why'* and unexplainable things began to happen to help us manifest our **dream**s.

The way we look at business is simple really... 1) find a problem, 2) come up with a solutions 3) package idea. Here are 5 steps that we find helpful:

1. To be successful you have to decide to change. If you want new results you have to do something different. 'YOU' must want to change, nothing will happen if your friends or family want you to change without you wanting to.

2. Take Action *NOW*: 'YOU' must **TAKE ACTION** - Set targets and give each one a completion deadline.

3. You have to commit 100%: There are a lot of options and they can distract your focus. 'YOU' must choose to commit to what's right for 'YOU'. What you are committed to and what you are interested in are completely different. For example: In a cheese burger, the 'BEEF' is committed and the 'CHICKEN is interested.

4. Stay Focused: Develop laser beam focus for your **dream**s and aspirations. There is no right or wrong way because there are pros and cons attached to each and every choice you make and be patient - little by little bit by bit. Only take part in activities and conversations that will bring you closer to having **FUN**, **DREAMING BIG** and making money doing what you **LOVE** *(((SMILE)))*.

5. Build strong relationships: Feed off positive input and spend quality time with people who

encourage, inspire and motivate you. Stand on the shoulders of giants and 'YOU' will observe more, because you will become like the three people who you spend most of your time with.

Our yummy mummy (Mrs Sabrina Ben Salmi BSc) was a lone parent. We moved home several times. We saw our mother go through a lot of difficulties. During difficult periods our mother taught us everything she learned including forgiveness. We have also seen our yummy mummy's ability to maintain focus on her **dream**s no matter how difficult things became this taught us so much. Mum had to overcome the stigma of lone parenthood and our grandmother has always remained a loyal and loving supporter. We **LOVE** our yummy grandmother very much because our mother could not have achieved so much without our grandmother helping when our yummy mummy had to work very hard. Mum has attracted some amazing support and wonderful friends. We have been taught to **LOVE** ourselves, others and to pursue our **dream**s no matter what *(((SMILE)))*. We have also been taught not to seek validation from others, and to simply believe in ourselves and to support each other as a family. It is our **dream** to see you find who you really are, your passion and ultimately assist you to have **FUN**, **DREAM BIG** and make money doing what you **LOVE**.

Did you know that your supreme asset is your existing passion, combined with your positive learnings gained from past experiences, your raw skills and more importantly your personal story? Yes or Yes? Your hobbies and interest are not meaningless no, no, no!... Every single thing that happens in your life happens for a purpose. Just know that every single thing that you have ever experienced made you who you are today. The results in your life are a result of past beliefs and actions; the good news is that you can intentionally create new results. All your experiences are all part of a **big**ger plan to contribute to making you unique, to enable you to add value to the world... You possess the ability to get yourself into any state you desire and create a life rich in having **FUN, DREAMING BIG** and making money doing what you **LOVE**. We encourage you to intentionally choose to get into a state of creativity when reading this book.

WE BELIEVE IN YOU AND IT IS ABOUT TIME THAT YOU START TO BELIEVE IN YOURSELF NOW (((SMILE)))!

xxx Ask your school and community centre to book a "Kidz that DREAM BIG" workshop xxx

HOW DOES THIS RELATE TO YOU?

DIARY ENTRIES

Dear Diary   21.1.2008

"Angle Cakes"

Angle Cakes - OMG! That's a cute name for a three year old, but I'm thirteen now. How on earth could my parents do this to me?

At school they call me carrot cake, because I have brown and orange freckles and my surname is Cakes. I don't pay them too much attention because I have the best time with my BFs (Charlie & Elizabeth) designing dresses etc. When we grow up our **dream** is to become famous fashion designers and own our very own boutique in Paris right next to the Eiffel Tower, we want to call it A.C.E. which is the first initials of our first names. School life can be tough if you choose focus on negativity. The three of us are not at all popular in school, but we enjoy each others company very much and keep our heads in our books. The three of us gel well together as we just focus on creating opportunities to make our **dream**s become a reality (((**SMILE**))) OMG!... when we talk about our **dream**s it's as if we are already living it. Our peers constantly make **fun** of us every day. I can't really put my feelings into words. Deep down inside we just know that our will come true, we don't know when or who but we do have a **big** why?..

Dear Diary   21.1.2017

Dreams do come true... I am now in my 20's and I am writing this diary entry from A.C.E our boutique in Paris, can you believe it? We are located right next to the Eiffel Tower in Paris. Wooooohoooo words can not explain how amazing we feel about living our **dream**s. The journey has been and continues to be absolutely amazing, the more we spoke about our **dream**s; crazy and unexplainable things happened to bring us closer to our **dream**s "I AM A CREATOR". We worked with different coaches at different stages of our journey. Woo hoo to date the magic continues to happen. We still have some distance to cover, however we are very proud of ourselves to have made it this far. It has taken a lot of focus, commitment and valued support from each other. One thing for sure, we have learned that when you maintain faith, **(((DREAMS)))** DO COME TRUE.

DRIP DROP POEM

Drip, drop, drip, drop........
I run down the window......
As a single pure seed and when connected I begin to grow.

Drip, drop, drip, drop........
I'm invincible, I can move through form and out of form based upon my hearts desire.

Drip, drop, drip, drop........
Although there are millions of rain drops on the window, I stand as one and I am unique.....

Drip, drop, drip, drop........

One day my drip, drop, drip, drop may appear to be gone, however the trail I leave behind shall always be remembered. What trail will your drip, drop, drip, drop be remembered for? What seed will you plant today?

A BIG CHANGE *(((SMILE)))*

Once upon a time there were two families, the North family who were financially free and the South family who were working class. The North family did not appreciate what they had. The parents and children simply showed off by constantly talking about their latest purchases and did not appreciate their privileged lifestyle, friends or family. The South family were very different. The parents taught their children to express gratitude for absolutely everything for example: their, health, their money, their clothing, their friends, family and opportunities etc. Everyday they spent quality time together talking about their values, beliefs, **dream**s and (((**PAYING IT FORWARD**))). They applied for grants and spoke to people about their ideas and they also made every effort to earn money and make their money work for them. Both families were neighbours, one day the South family invited the North family over for dinner... The North family laughed at the South family and rejected their invitation because they felt that they were better than the South family. A few years later the South families lives began to change, nothing that was noticeable to outsiders but they felt that their beliefs were positively shifting. A few more years past and the South family began displaying visible changes. The North family experienced huge financial losses and they had to purchase a smaller home and sell their family cars etc. Slowly their lifestyle began to change. The North family became working class and the South family became wealthy in abundance. The South family who eventually became financially and time free maintained appreciation for everything in their lives and now they share their secrets to wealth with others. The North family who became working class approached the South family and asked what the secret was to their wealth? The South family invited them to dinner and this time the North family accepted. During dinner they spoke about having **FUN**, **dream**ing **big**, making money doing what you **LOVE** and more importantly the attitude of gratitude and ... **(((SMILE)))** what else do you believe to be the secret to wealth, heath and happiness in abundance?

You do know right? Yes or Yes - What are you pretending not to know in order to believe that you don't know?

(Tray-Séan, me and Stedman Grahman (Educator, author and the partner of media mogul Oprah Winfrey)

BE THE BEST YOU CAN BE

Convert your adversity into empowerment right here and right NOW. We believe that if you want to be the best you can be – it'll benefit you to create a pitch, build a network, convey gratitude, find a coach/mentor, build your profile, publish a book and create products/services. Allow us to explain in a little more details:

- Pitch = know and communicate your message to your target audience with a burning desire.

- Network = in business it is not what you know or who you know that counts. What counts most is who knows you. Create and build good relationships with people who you like and trust, because this will enable you to gain exclusive JVs (joint ventures).

- Gratitude = always show gratitude for others, your health and opportunities. Respect will help you in your journey.

- Mentor/Coach = seek and you shall find... Get a coach, because a coach will expand yor boundary conditions etc. Find someone who you would like to become or at least learn from.

- Profile = if you can't be found on the internet the chances are that people will not feel you are credible. What comes up when you type your name into any search engine? Create a trail leading to you and your mission.

- Publish = this changes everything... when you become an author you gain credibility and visibility. The word author = authority *(((SMILE)))* writing a book is so much **FUN**

- Product = convert your knowledge, experience and skills into products for example: Books, Apps, Sweets, Cakes, DVDs, CDs, games etc

(left our friend Alena, Mayor of Redbridge, me in the middle, Mayoress and Tray-Séan)

BEING YOU IS A PIECE OF CAKE POEM

It's good being **ME**!....

I am happy being **ME** and not trying to be someone else, because I AM special and **LOVED**. That's why being **ME** is a piece of cake.

It is very important to learn to **LOVE** myself and be proud of myself about trying my best.

Being **ME** is always easier, because it is a piece of cake being **ME**.

I always try to do my best no matter what and set a good example for my peers by simply being **ME**.

Well done for acknowledging how special YOU are xxx (((SMILE))) xxx

Always know that you are precious and loved dearly. FYI the fact that you are alive means that you are special.

(Tray-Séan and I)

SHOW RESPECT FOR YOUR LIFE AND OTHERS

We believe that God has given us life, so we ought to have respect for our own life, environment and others. Having respect for life includes having the right view of our elders, peers, environment etc. You need to root out of your heart any hatred, jealousy and anger because this will only cause negativity. If you have respect for life, you will keep in mind positivity and you would not be careless and will not take risks for pleasure or excitement. You will avoid reckless, violent or dangerous activities. A good intention is always a good starting point. Keep your environment clean at all times to avoid accidents so someone does not trip, fall and get badly hurt. Simply ensure that your actions inspire and empower others instead of being harmful to yourself or others.

Being cruel to animals or killing them is wrong and shows disregard for the sacredness of life. You must learn to **LOVE** others, support others and respect yourself, others and your family, friends, peers, elders and environment.

SOLACE

If for any reason you're finding comfort in negative or unfulfilling behaviour? The chances are you're beating yourself up about it. This will only make things worse, we encourage you to replace your negative and unfulfilling behaviour with positive and fulfilling ones. Every choice you make has an advantage and disadvantage associated to it. Positive and fulfilling behaviour will assist your development and unfulfilling behaviour will not. We suggest that you develop your gift of '**intentionality**'. Make it your obligation to pursue k**now**ledge without interference, preserve the positive learnings and surround yourself with people who you like and trust. Do this and you will find comfort in more fulfilling activities and you will begin to manifest your **dream**s. Through expanded awareness and preserving the positive learnings your k**now**ledge will increase and your model of the world will change. Then you will begin to experience your body and reality in new ways, beyond your wildest **dream**s.

Your supreme mind harnesses infinite power, the universe is teaming with infinite possibilities and you are one way which the universe has chosen to express it's self. FYI you are so **PRECIOUS** and **LOVED**, more than words can explain! We challenge you to take a good look at society; you will see the need for a paradigm shift because there is a lack of: **LOVE**, peer-to-peer support, self-worth, gratitude, unity and empathy. Modern materialism has striped us of the need to feel responsible. It is our belief that you have been conditioned to believe that you have no control of your internal world (your mind) and external world (your environment). The truth is you are the master of your mind and each and every one of us is uniquely influencing the world which we see.

Aggression and over eating and other unfulfilling behaviours are signs of emotional emptiness. We encourage you to pay close attention to your actions because they tell you a lot about the emotional state you are in:

- If you continue to do what you already know... how will you create new results?

In order to remedy the root cause of a problem, be sympathetic with 'yourself'. Trust yourself and set out to discover the deeper need that the unfulfilling behaviour is satisfying? Once you have established the root cause simply replace the unfulfilling behaviour with a fulfilling behaviour, one which makes you feel good about yourself.

Good or Bad Emotions

We have been taught that emotions are neither good nor bad, it is the addiction which courses you problems because you become physiologically and biochemically attached to let's say: sadness, aggression anger or over eating. Your addiction causes you to create scenarios which will trigger the release of the specific peptide which you are addicted to. Continuously remind yourself that you deserve to be **HAPPY**, **LOVED** and **RESPECTED** or better... Right?... Yes or Yes?

Learn to **LOVE** yourself and everything will fall into place eventually. Now we want you to think of a problem which is causing you to feel sad, jealous, aggressive, anger or over eating and answer the following questions:

- What is the problem?

- What is not the problem?

- What will need to happen in order to gain your desired outcome?

- How will you know when you have overcome the solution to that old problem?

- When will you **STOP!** That old problem from being a limitation?

Now visualise yourself in some indefinite time in the future and notice how that old problem is no longer an issue and notice how positively different your life is now.

What will you choose to create now? After all you are a creator right? Yes or Yes? (((SMILE)))

OBEY YOUR PARENT(S)/GAURDIAN(S)

We can totally understand that from time to time you may find it hard to obey your parent(s) or guardian(s). You should appreciate their guidance because you will grow to understand why they say or do what they do in time. Put yourself in their shoes to help you to understand their perspective. Simply obey your parent(s)/guardian(s) even when it is difficult circumstances. There have been times when our yummy mummy asked us to do something that was especially hard because it meant that we would loose what appeared to be a good thing at the time. We did what was requested because we know that our yummy mummy **LOVES** us dearly and wants the best for us. OMG! Lol! FYI.. That wasn't always the case, because like you there were times when we rebelled and did not agree with what we were told to do. There may be times when you do not see your parent(s)/guardian(s) point of view, but we encourage you to just obey because you know that they only want to protect you and more importantly they know best.

We both know that you are often subject to peer pressure and tempted to do what is wrong just to appear cool in front of friends (which can often be hard to resist). This is why it is very important for you to surround yourself with friends you like and trust instead of surrounding yourself with wrongdoers, because they will simply led you into a lot of trouble.

- How might your parent(s)/guardian(s)/, friends or family feel if you were to become involved in any form of unlawful immoralities?

Only disobey your parent(s)/guardian(s) if they ask you to do something that is unlawful, violent or any other dangerous or unfulfilling act. If this happens try to teach your parent(s)/guardian(s) with **LOVE** and explain why the unlawful, violent or any other dangerous or unfulfilling act may be potentially damaging for your development.

MUSIC

Did you know that *MUSIC* appeals to your ever emotion. It soothes and excites you, uplifts and inspires you. It moves you to happiness and reduces you to tears because music speaks directly to your hearts.

- Can you imagine life without music?

- Have you ever wondered how different genre of music influences your mood or actions?

- What is your favourite genre of music and how does it make you feel when you listen to it?

- Observe your friends, family and other people you know. Observe the music they listen to and how do you think that genre of music influences their mood or behaviour?

- Have you ever noticed how some music makes you feel playful, aggressive or even sad?

Music is a beautiful gift from God and it is one that people around the world treasure. Music is available to millions of people across the world at our finger tips. A verity of music can be recorded, downloaded and played on a verity of devices that can be slipped into your pocket. So much has changed since your parents were young. Please be very careful of the genre of music you listen to – listen to the words very, very, very carefully because it effects your emotions.

LEARN TO LOVE 'YOU'

Childhood and Adolescence can present a range of fear provoking and exhilarating thoughts! It is entirely normal to experience mixed emotions from time to time. There will be days when you feel: confident, playful and happy. There will also be days when you feel: sad, discontent and miserable. Days when you are not feeling 100% - it's particularly important to wear a huge (((**SMILE**)))! Be kind and loving towards yourself just as you would be towards **LOVED** ones. Do things to make you feel good for example listen to music, talk to friends and family, draw, look into a mirror and appreciate yourself, write, laugh, read or exercise - whatever makes you feel good JUST DO IT!

Express gratitude for your life and praise yourself for all of your achievements. For example you could say "I am so proud of myself for: completing my home work, helping out around the house or reading a book". Whatever it is (((**CELEBRATE**))) your achievements.

These sentences can help to make you feeling good:

- I **LOVE** being me
- I **LOVE** my life
- I **LOVE** my perfect body
- I **LOVE** being healthy
- I am the man (for boys only Lol!)
- I am beautiful (for girls only Lol!)
- I **LOVE** my happiness and sooooooooooo much more
- I **LOVE** being ME... I **LOVE** being ME... I **LOVE** being ME...! YIPPEE! YIPPEE! YIPPEE!

(((**SMILE**))) I **LOVE** my life...

IMPROVE RELATIONSHIPS NOW (((SMILE)))

Tray-Séan and I are the oldest of four; we have a junior sister named Yasmine and a junior brother named Mohamed-Salah (aka Paolo). Woooo hooo Lol! Do we have good **fun** with them LOL!... that's an understatement! If they are not getting us into trouble, they are giving us kisses and cuddles followed by messing up our rooms and breakings our belongings or telling tails **(((SMILE)))**. Tray-Séan and I have had disagreements too. We know that it is common for siblings to disagree from time-to-time. We often disagree LOL! LOL! LOL! **(((SMILE)))** It's okay to disagree at times, we have learned to respect each other's model of the world and opinions – let's just say we are working on it... LOL! LOL! LOL! **(((SMILE)))**. When we spend quality time together enjoying our common interests we get on just fine.

Did you know that you can change your life by improving the quality of the relationships you have with yourself and others by simply improving your communication skills.

We are The Ben Salmi Duo and we are here to remind you that there are some things guaranteed in life and one of them is **(((CHANGE)))**

Take a moment to think about the different relationships in your life and answer the following questions:

- Do you tell them that you appreciate them?

- Do you enjoy their company?

- Do you share your **dream**s and aspirations with them?
- Do you ask them what their **dream**s and aspirations are?
- Do you respect their values and beliefs with them?
- Do you talk to each other or at each other?
- Do you fully understand them?
- Do you make them feel as if there is something worthwhile in them?
- Do you treat them the way you want to be treated?
- Do you criticise them?

Preserve the positive learnings.

The good news is if you want to improve a relationships you simply to working on '**YOU**':

- Compliment them and ask questions about them to show that you are interested in them
- Listen when spoken to and give them eye contact
- Respond with empathy and use their name during conversations
- Talk about them instead of talking about yourself

If you want to improve a relationship it is always a good idea to be clear about what you want to improve. These questions will help you to get clear about the type of relationship you want:

- What do you want to improve about the relationship?

- How will you k**now** the relationship has improved?

- What will you need to change about you **now** in order to achieve your desired outcome(s)?

- Notice how the old problem use to hold back the development of the relationship, how are you starting to see things differently **now**?

- How do you k**now**?

Go ahead and preserve the positive learnings.

YOU CAN CHANGE YOUR LIFE

Did you know that your values and beliefs are learned from a combination of your family, friends, religion, school, geography, demographics, economics, media and significant emotional events.

- Do you know how powerful your brain is?

- Do you k**now** how your unconscious minds absorb information from birth?

Between the ages of 0-7 your brain is like a sponge and you copy whatever you are exposed to. This is known as the 'Imprint Period'. Between the ages of 7-14 you begin to select role models and this is k**now**n as the 'Modelling Period'. Between the ages of 14-21 you choose a group to belong to. It is fair to say that this group became your life advisory board in many ways. This is k**now**n as the 'Socialization Period'. Between the ages of 21-35 is when you would have gathered a collection of experiences as a result of all of the above. It is believed that to some extent your 'Business Persona' resembles your first boss of authority figure. This is known as the 'Business Persona Period'.

- Have you ever heard about the 'Hierarchy of Change'? If your answer is no, we encourage you to do some research.

Just sit back and relax and allow us to explain... well at least what we've been taught LOL! (((**SMILE**)))

It is human nature to protect your identity; an identity shift will change your life, because your identity forms who you are. Values determine where you spend your time. Whatever you value most you will take pride in, because it is important to you.

- Did you know, where your attention goes, energy flows and results will show?

Your beliefs are possibilities which you believe to be true. Your beliefs are 'Your Boundary Conditions'. Your beliefs change your capabilities, behaviour and the environment you choose to be in. Change your beliefs and you can change your life. Your capabilities are influenced by your behaviour. When you enhance your capabilities your behaviour will improve and change will happen. Your behaviour is influenced by your capabilities, and will affect the environment which you choose to be in. Changing your environment has less of an impact on changing your life because it is a superficial change because it is not deep rooted enough to cause a significant change.

Woooooohooooo! We hope you took that all in (((**SMILE**))) take a moment to think about these questions:

- Where do you believe you learned some of your behaviours from?

The good news is, if you learned unfulfilling behaviours. You can choose to learn more fulfilling ones right? Yes or Yes?

- Did you k**now** that your brain processes information using representational systems after receiving data from your five senses?

These are sight, sound, touch, taste, smell and self-talk. Your brain translates the external world into an internal representation of your own unique reality, as we all have our own interpretation of reality.

- Can you remember the last movie you watched with friends or family member?

If you ask them what their interpretation was. The chances are that you both had totally different interpretation of the same movie - right? Yes or Yes? But you both watched the same movie. This is because your individual internal filters are different and this influences your interpretation of the external world are different. Your internal filters are constantly changing and they are different for each of us. We challenge you to watch the same movie a few times, each time you do you will notice something different because your awareness expands each and every time.

There are many things that affect you each and every day, the music you listen to, the language you use and the environments you are in, what goes on in your head and the images you are exposed to etc.

Our yummy mummy often gives us this example. Visualise adding: Eggs, Butter, Flour, Sugar and Water into a mixing bowl. Then mix it all together and place it into the oven:

- Would you be surprised to find that you've baked a cake?

Now reflect on your own life, if for any reason you're surrounded by negative role models, negative language, disrespect, lack, struggle, negative media, negative images, negative experiences, negative music or negative people etc. The outcome is what is currently showing up in your life today. Your values and beliefs are the mental constructs of your thoughts, ideas and opinions that you hold to be true about yourself, the world around you and people etc.

These internal filters determine your behaviour and totally influence the way you experience your life. Woooohoooo... The good news is that you simply learned a recipe to cook your way to this point in your life. This means that you can learn a new recipe to create a life filled with having **FUN, DREAMING BIG** and making money doing what you **LOVE**. We don't **know** if you are going to get this immediately, or when you sleep. What we do **know** is that you will get it – right? Yes or Yes? We are The Ben Salmi Duo, and we are still having **fun** learning (((**SMILE**))).

It is easy to understand why our parent(s)/guardian(s) are so worried and anxious about our development, wellbeing and safety. Society has become complicated, hectic and dangers have also increase. Our parent(s)/guardian(s) will automatically do their best to keep us out of harm's way. The responsibilities of loving parent(s)/guardian(s) never end, whether it's looking out for your best interests or simply being there for support, all children and youth desire unconditional **LOVE**.

You have unbounded potential, you can choose to create whatever you desire to experience. The only thing blocking your view from seeing this unbounded potential is your 'SET OF BELIEFS'. Your 'SET OF BELIEFS' are the reason why you only see or experience a polarised view of what you call reality. The good news is that your 'SET OF BELIEFS' are entirely made up – yes that's right! They are totally made up. It is very important for you to fully understand what we are saying, because your understanding of this will change your life. Your beliefs are simply a mental construct of your thoughts, ideas and opinions which you hold to be true about yourself, people and your surrounding world and they are extremely powerful. They influence your behaviour and totally control the way you experience life.

Hear us when we say that your values and beliefs are picked up from experiences you encounter, significant emotional events and people who influence you etc. Most of your values and beliefs probably didn't originate from your own thinking. You more than likely inherited them from your family, culture, education, environment and friends etc. However you believe your values and beliefs to be the truth right?... You may not even be conscious of these beliefs because they operate in your subconscious mind. Whilst many of these beliefs create positive life enhancing behaviours and give positive experiences – but some don't. Instead they cause negative, unproductive and sometimes destructive behaviours and experiences. Because your beliefs operate in your unconscious mind, it may appear as if things happen to you without you having any control over your life, and that the results you get are random, that's not the case. IT'S TIME TO AWAKE **now** - you have been conditioned to forget that values and beliefs are made up. The good news is that you can change your negative and disempowering values and beliefs to ones which will allow you to have **FUN**, **DREAM BIG** and make money doing what you **LOVE** right now if you are willing? You have the power to reinvent yourself so that you are all you wish to be, do and have – right **now**. When you change your values and beliefs, your thoughts, feelings, actions will change too and new results will begin to show in your life. Some changes will be instant and other changes will begin to show over time so be patient because it's going to take commitment, focus and unwavering faith to transform your values and beliefs. Wooooohooooo just relax and know that all will be well (((**SMILE**))).

Slow down; slow down one step at a time! So today, right here, right **now** – we want you to take a deep breath. Remember the lifestyle you experience today has been cooking for many years. You may be financially healthy or you may be financially trapped. What we want you to fully consider are the questions below:

- What recipe(s) did you use to get here?

- Who taught you the recipe(s)?

- Are you ready to learn new recipes – ones that will taste mouth-watering?

- Are you willing to commit?

- Are you willing to do whatever it takes to have **FUN**, **DREAM BIG** and make money doing what you **LOVE**?

- Are you ready to play? Yes or Yes?

Woooo hoooo awesome... this process can be **FUN**, and the rewards can be huge too. **Now** take a moment to think about these questions:

- What values and beliefs do you have about yourself, life, others, opportunities and the world that are stopping you having what you want?
- What values and beliefs cause you to be in a state of unhappiness, sadness, and discontent and leaving you feeling stuck in your life?

When something appears to be taken from you, just k**now** that you are not being punished. K**now** that in order for something positive to enter into your life, adequate space needs to be made. You are simply being prepared to receive something better. Just k**now** that you have exactly what it takes to overcome whatever may come your way. STOP! Waiting to be rescued, WAKE UP! You are the **one** you've been waiting for! You have the power to transform your life right here, right **now** – with this book… if you are willing. FYI **YOU** are the **one** who is going to make 'it' happen – right? Yes or Yes?

Are you ready to play? Yes or Yes?

Create a table that looks like the one below; in each column insert at least 10 values that are important to you in connection to the following areas: Life, Business or Career and Relationships please see the example below:

LIFE	BUSINESS/CAREER	RELATIONSHIPS
Health	Success	Trust
GRATITUDE	Social impact	Honesty
LOVE	Profit	Respect
Family	Team	Communication

Awesome **now** it's your turn… imagine your brain is like the World Wide Web – whatever you type into the search engine, results relating to your search topic will be presented. We challenge you to have **FUN**, **DREAM BIG** and make money doing what you **LOVE**.

- If you can seek and discover something amazing, why settle for anything less?

Visualise being in a super market. Walk down the aisles and look on the shelves that have: Bread, milk and eggs. Look at all of the verities to choose from, nowadays there are so many options to choose from:

- Bread: Gluten-free, wholemeal, white, organic and brown to name a few

- Eggs: organic, barn, farm and free-range to name a few

- Milk: skimmed, semi-skimmed, whole and organic to name a few

Because there's so much to choose from our parent(s)/guardian(s) usually create a shopping list. Lol! Otherwise they'll simply go shopping for one item and leave after purchasing several products which they didn't intend to purchase. Ha! Ha! Ha! Our yummy mummy used to fall victim to store marketing tricks too, so your parent(s)/guardian(s) are not alone **(((SMILE)))**. We challenge you to create a life shopping list for all areas of your life. This will help you to reduce your chances of picking up undesirable life experiences, businesses, and relationships and so on. This will help you to get clear about what you really want.

Always remember that life is not a sprint. We believe that life is more like taking part in a marathon; slow and steady wins the race. More importantly go at your own pace! Yeah there will be ups and downs, and at times you will be full of energy and at other times you might lack the will to go on. Some times the sun might shine and at times the wind may blow. There may be times when it may rain for a while. Just maintain focus each and every time you feel like giving up. During periods of difficulty, we encourage you to praise yourself for how far you have come and how little distance you have left to go to reach the finishing line.

During the marathon some supporters will remain by your side from the start to finish, some will stay a short while and others will come and go. Some may dishearten you and others will say exactly what you need to hear in order for you to get a boost of energy.

Hey let's face it they'll be 101 reasons to doubt your ability to triumph. However your **big** 'why' will empower you to do whatever it takes to ensure that you remain motivated. Just when you feel like giving up you will have to dig deep, because you k**now** that it will all be worthwhile in the end. Once you have accomplished your desired outcome(s) – right? Yes or Yes? (((**SMILE**))):

- What values and beliefs would you like to learn?

- How will adopting new values and beliefs change your life?

- Analyse your values and beliefs and if for any reason something appears to be missing simply ask yourself why and ack**now**ledge how it has affected your life?

For example many people forget to list values like: money, health, wealth, happiness or paying it forward etc. Then realise why money, health, wealth, happiness etc have been lacking or totally absent in their life (((**SMILE**))). Remember there are no wrong or right answers. It's your life so you be the judge. What positive learnings did you discover about yourself, values and beliefs?

THE MONEY GAME

Unfortunately our schools do not teach us financial education and how to have **FUN** with money. Rest assure because the Ben Salmi Duo are here to play... You are a money magnet right? Yes or Yes?

You will need 7 money boxes or containers to play this game. Oh yeah we almost forgot to mention, this game will never end... The better you get at playing it the more **FUN** you will have with it (((SMILE))).

Make sure that the money boxes are all the same size; now label each money box or container AS FOLLOWS in bold text:

- ➤ **EDUCATIONAL** = 5% each month use what you have saved for educational materials e.g. training, books etc

- ➤ **PAY IT FORWARD** = 5% each month use what you have saved to donate to charity or help a family or individual less fortunate

- ➤ **ESSENTIALS** = 50% each month use what you have saved to purchase essential items or pay for essential bills e.g. mobile top up, clothing etc

- ➤ **SPEND ME** = 10% use this money for general spending

- ➤ **INVESTMENTS** = 10% each month put this money into your bank account and when it grows to a large amount use it to invest in new business ideas and or investments

- **HAVE FUN** = 10% each month use what you have saved to treat yourself to whatever you want. You have to spend this one each and every month because if you are not having **FUN** you will not get better at this game.

- **DREAM BIG & MAKE MONEY DOING WHAT YOU LOVE** = 10% never ever, ever, ever, ever spend this money. You must put this money into your saving account each and every month. Never ever spend this as you grow up you with drawn a monthly allowance and live of the interest only.

Whenever you get pocket money simply divide it into the 7 money boxes or containers. It would be fun for you to teach your parent(s)/guardian(s) this game.

Example: If you have £20 you will put the following amount into each one: EDUCATIONAL = £1 PAY IT FORWARD = £1 10% ESSENTIALS = **£10** SPENDING ME = £2 INVESTMENTS = £2 HAVE **FUN** = £2
 DREAM BIG & MAKE MONEY DOING WHAT YOU **LOVE** = £2

Woo hoo! Awesome – here's to your success and creating a life filled with having *FUN*, *DREAMING BIG* and making money doing what you *LOVE.*

EMOTIONS

FYI! If for any reason you are trying to resist uncomfortable emotions they will not go away. We always believe that it's better to express instead of repress emotions, otherwise you'll simply increase the negative energy wishing that the emotion would go away. If you dwell on how unpleasant it makes you feel or worry that it might get worse, you will not be able to think straight. By simply saying out aloud how you desire to feel, you will be amazed, because it can have a strange phenomenon of diminishing the unwanted emotion.

- Are you ready to PLAY? Yes or Yes?

Now! We want you to focus on and fully experience the uncomfortable emotion. This may seem a little unpleasant; just relax and embrace your emotion now. It will benefit you to face up to your uncomfortable emotion. **Now** answer these questions:

- What do you find uncomfortable about the emotion?

- Is it really so terrible that you can't confront it **now**?

- What is the problem?

- What is not the problem?

- That was a terrible problem wasn't it?

If you can face up to your emotions **now**... please go ahead and do so. Just k**now** that it's okay to experience your uncomfortable emotion for **now**, because it will help you to release the negative energy and you will become (((FREE))) to continue your journey of having **fun**, **dream**ing **big** and making money doing what you **love**.

That's right..... Just relax and fully experience your emotions.

If you feel like crying – cry... just do it! If you feel like expressing yourself through writing - write... **Just Do It!** If you feel like shouting - shout... **Just Do It!** And if you feel like talking - talk... **Just Do It!** Just let your emotions to flow freely. Do whatever you feel like doing **Just Do It! Now**, just go ahead and relax; it is okay to express your emotions **now**. Take a deep breath!... and relax

WELL DONE!!! WE RESPECT YOUR COURAGE (((SMILE)))

The fact that you are reading this book means, that you are ready to create a life filled with a wealth of having **FUN**, **DREAM**ING **BIG** and making money doing what you **LOVE**.

Preserve the positive learnings for yourself and for the future.

We believe that things happen either as a result of something we do or something we don't do in our lives. We also believe that all problems are problems of the mind and therefore all solutions are solutions of the mind. You are responsible for yourself and cannot control others, however you are responsible for the way you choose to respond or react to any given experience in your life journey. We also believe that the universe does not make mistakes and that everything happens for a reason, because of our beliefs we strongly feel that a problem well stated is a problem half solved. We always find it helpful to talk to our mother, grandmother and friends about how we are feeling. We are the Ben Salmi Duo and we believe that it is always good to talk about your feelings and experiences, because bottling it up inside is often worst than speaking to someone about your feelings and emotions.

Are You Ready To PLAY? Yes or Yes? We want you to think of a problem and then answer each of the following questions:

- What is the problem?

- What is the root cause of the problem?

- How have you failed to resolve this?

- How can you overcome the problem?

- What would you like to transform **now**?

- When will you stop it from being a limitation?

- How many ways do you k**now** you have solved this?

- How are you changing and seeing things differently **now**?

- How do you k**now**?

- That was a terrible problem wasn't it?

Now that you are seeing and understanding things differently it feels great... Right! Yes or Yes?

FYI! You are exactly where you need to be right **now**..... Preserve the positive learnings. OMG! (((**SMILE**))) Let's face it! It's your responsibility to gain positive learnings, for example you can lead a horse to the water but you can't make the horse drink unless the horse is willing.

This is a perfect opportunity for you to explore who you really are? That's right... a precious and unique opportunity to rediscover yourself and your true passion, values, beliefs and so much more.

Answer these questions:

- Who are you? LOL! No we don't mean... your name etc.

- We mean who are you?

- After all you are a divine child of God aren't you?

- You are the answer to many prays right? Yes or Yes?

- You are a creator right?

- How do you know?

- What do you want to create?

- What do you really want in all areas of your life?

We can appreciate that after years of being told that you are just a child and defining yourself as a 'son/daughter' or 'sister/brother' or 'pupil/child'. We can totally understand that you may have lost sight of who you truly are and what you truly desire.

At times in life you may fall along the way!

- What do you do when you fall down?

Yes, that's right! **Get back up...** In life there are times when you might feel like you just don't have the strength to **get back up**... It may even feel impossible to **get back up**...

- If you don't try to **get back up,** will you get up?

No... If you start to move your legs in the walking motion whilst laying flat on the ground

- Will you get anywhere?

No... So we encourage you to take control of your life and **get back up now**. We encourage you to keep trying no matter what. Just know that you will learn along the way and more importantly you will be taking steps closer to your **dream**s. Remember other children and youth are always observing you... and your courage will inspire them to do the same or better. From today promise yourself; if you fall 1000 times you will get up 1000 times. It doesn't matter how many times you fall what matters most is preserving the positive learnings, rising up empowered and finishing strong... right? Yes or Yes?

(Me and Ralph Plumb – woo hoo Ralph gifted me his very own money maker aka Blue Snowball)

I LOVE MY LIFE

Spend time rebuilding **YOU**, be someone who you would **LOVE** to spend time with. Be the first person to praise **YOU** when you triumph and the first person to tell yourself that there is no such thing as failure, only feedback! When things don't go according to plan... promise to see optimism in every situation which life presents and learn to say

"**I LOVE MY LIFE**" and "**I LOVE BEING ME**"

After all you are the master of your mind - right? Yes or Yes? Be the change you, you want to see and you will attract positive people, events, experiences, opportunities and much more to you. Spend time improving yourself, leaving **no time to criticise others**. It will also benefit you to be as enthusiastic about the success of others as you are about your own and (((**SMILE**))) cheerfully throughout your day.

Remember the most important relationship you will ever have in your entire life is the one you have with **YOURSELF**. As we have said before the quality of this relationship defines absolutely everything within all areas of your life, learning to (((**LOVE YOU**))) is an internal gesture and only you hold the key. LOL! LOL! We understand that this is going to take practice, time, commitment and patience. If for any reason you find it slightly challenging, simply visualize talking to a **LOVED ONE**. Don't worry because it will be a piece of cake - you can do it... right? Yes or Yes? Please promise to be gentle, kind and have empathy with yourself. Remember, where your attention goes, energy flows and results will begin to show within all areas of your life (((**SMILE**))). We have a positive mantra to share with you: "I **LOVE** to think positively, I **LOVE** to speak positively, I **LOVE** to act positively and I **LOVE** to feel positively (((**SMILE**)))

YOU ARE UNIQUE

You are often misguided by the media, music and society. There are many things that you may believe simply because of what you see, hear or read. You only have to open your eyes and take a good look at society. We are all unique, and the ***BEN SALMI DUO*** believes that diversity is (((AWESOME))).

Can you imagine how life would be if everything and everyone were the same? It is about you learned to **LOVE** yourself and others unconditionally. You know that so much of the stuff you learn from school, newspapers, society and in the media is sometimes pointless... right? Yes or Yes? Where are the stuff about; financial education, emotional education, peer-to-peer support, sharing ideas, networking, cooperative living, entrepreneurship, accepting differences, celebrating diversity, understanding and unconditional **LOVE**?

You are a ***CREATOR***, and you have the ability to dance with the universe, create huge ripple effects of positivity and inspire other children and youth across the globe to do the same or better (((**SMILE**))). You have a story to share and the ability to teach others. There are children and youth waiting to be touched by your positive vibrations. Don't buy into the hoax of having to have 'X' or be 'X' in order to be perfect. The **fact that you are alive is confirmation of how amazing you are**. Be proud of who you are and your qualities rather than your so called flaws or differences. Focus on your skills, passion, purpose, positive learnings, abilities and qualities. Boys **you are the man** and girls **you are beautiful, worthy and unique**. If you don't believe it yet... simply, feel the feelings of being just that. *Now* go to a mirror and appreciate **YOU** by saying:

"I LOVE my life, I have skills, I have a passion, I have a purpose, I have valuable positive learnings to share with others, I have chosen to convert my adversity into empowerment... right here right now, and I have the ability and qualities to pursue my dreams because I am a creator and the master of my mind. Therefore I choose to create a life filled with a wealth of health, wealth and happiness. I am LOVED and valued dearly - being me is a piece of cake. I want to have FUN, DREAM BIG and make money doing what I LOVE now (((SMILE)))." Wooo hooo

Don't just take our word for it – try it yourself and you be the judge (((**SMILE**))). The *Ben Salmi Duo* is passionate about community cohesion; and we strongly believe that we should all unite because we only have one life as we k**no**w it. So we should express respect and gratitude for life and each other.

(Me and Robert G Allen)

HARMONIOUS

Getting clear about what you want is essential when setting out to accomplish your ***dreams***. If you don't take the time to get clear about what you want it will simply limit your chances of achieving your ***dreams***.

Our yummy mummy has taught us that in the absence of clarity, you will either roam without direction or you will create a life filled with results which you don't feel good about. You might experience joyful experiences, but the end result often falls short of your initial intention, this can leave you with a sinking feeling in your stomach...

Hey do you ever look at your life and think to yourself "How on earth did I get here?", "I'm bored!" don't worry it has happened to us too so you are not alone. If for any reason you are thinking... "If setting goals is so important, why are so few children and youth actually doing it?" We believe that part of the reason is because of a lack of awareness and **know**ledge about how to set goals. Have you ever wondered why we go through years of schooling and never receive any formal instructions on how to goal set. Once you **know** what you want, you may even surprise yourself by exceeding your initial expectation(s). Do you fail to take action because you fear making a so called mistake or so called failing or are you simply too scared that your friends may make **fun** of? If so, **STOP!** Remember it is the **taking action that counts most**. We are here to remind you, that there is no such thing as failure - only feedback. **Now** ask yourself what would you do if you weren't afraid? We encourage you to shift your focus and remember how many times you found the courage to get up after you fell instead of how many times you fell. Whenever you want to get clarity about what you really want, don't listen to what you say. Instead pay close attention to what you do, that will tell you what you really want.

Now think about these questions:

- What do you need to stop doing?

- What do you need to do less of?

- What do you need to start doing?

- What do you need to do more of?

Set daily reminders on your electronic device or write these questions in your diary.

You k**now** that actions, speaks louder than words... right? Yes or Yes? So promise yourself that you will ***TAKE ACTION NOW!....***

YOU ARE THE MASTER OF YOUR MIND!...

If you want to think positive thoughts, first you must feel positive. Be very, very, very careful of the language you use and the thoughts you have. We know that it might seem cool to copy friends. However always pay close attention to your inner negative voice that dismisses any good idea you have.
YOU THINK POSITIVELY! YOU SPEAK POSITIVELY! YOU ACT POSITIVELY! YOU FEEL POSITIVELY!

If you don't master your mind, the chances are that your mind will master you! My brother and I often say this mantra: "I am the master of my mind because I choose to be". As you continue to read, you may notice a voice in your head... become familiar with its tone and the type of language you hear - for example: "You're not good enough", "I'm not good enough", "I can't do that", "You don't need to do that", "It is too difficult to do 'X' because I am too young", "I don't have support", "I am not educated", "You look fat in that", "I'll never figure out a plan", "Who do you think you are?", "What's the point?", "I'm not in the mood", "I'll do it later" and "You can't do that, be that, have - that... because.... because.... because....". You might think that this voice runs on autopilot and most of the time you may be totally unaware of it. The good news is that you can take control of that voice in your head, right here and right **now**.

- Did you know that all change takes place on an unconscious level because change takes place internally then results begin to show externally?

For example visualise planting an apple tree... do you plant a huge tree or a seed? When you plant a seed the apple tree does not appear as soon as you plant the seed. First the seed begins to change in the soil and then the results begin to show when it grows out of the soil.

It is very, very, very important for you to replace your old disempowering voice with more empowering one now... for example "You are good enough", "I'm good enough", "I can do that", "I'll do it **now**", "I do need to do that **now**", "I do have support", "I am educated", "You look fab-u-lous in that....", "It is because I am a young, I have to do 'X' to create the life I deserve and inspire other young people", "You can do that , be that, have that, "I think I am the right person to do X", "There's many reason to do this", "I'm the master of my mind and I choose to be happy **now**" and "I will figure out a plan because....because....because".

We have been taught that how you do one thing, is how you do everything. For example if you do not take action in one area of your life, the chances are when an opportunity presents you will not to take action. This is because this is how you have chosen to program yourself; we could call it a habitual action.

- Did you know that how you choose to think about anything creates the experience you will have of that very thing?

Change your thinking and you change your life! By simply exchanging your disempowering (negative) thoughts into empowering (positive) alternatives **now,** you will be on the road to creating a life filled with having **FUN**, **DREAMING BIG** and making money doing what you **LOVE**. Remember it does not matter how much or how little you start with, what matters most is what you choose to do right here and right **now**.

We believe in you and it's about time that you start to believe in yourself right here and right **now**.

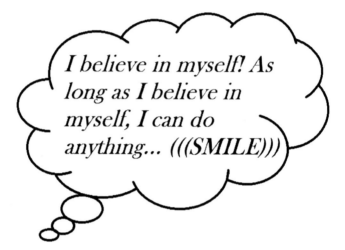

CONVERT YOUR ADVERSITY INTO EMPOWERMENT

Choose to convert your adversities into empowerment right here and right **now**:

- What do you want?

- What do you really want?

- What are you passionate about?

- What problem(s) have you found?

- What problem(s) are you going to solve with your product(s)/service(s)?

- What will you share with the world?

- What do you like to do to have **FUN**?

- What would you do right now if you weren't afraid to **DREAM BIG**?

- What could you create to make money doing what you **LOVE**?

FYI! We are here to tell you that it does not matter what anyone else thinks of you. What matters most is what you think of yourself. Come on get it together, the words that come from your mouth you're the first to hear. So speak words of positivity and you shall find yourself there. We have been taught that whatsoever you **dream**, you will experience (((**SMILE**))). You must... heal your mind, body and soul.

(((**CONGRATULATE**))) yourself right here and right **now** for each and every single thing that you have had to experience in order to arrive at this very point in your life. No one else can dance your dance; right now there are children and youth out there just waiting for you to share your story with them. You have a unique message in you, one that will touch the hearts and minds of sooooo many and your message will contribute to making the world a better place.

Just know that you are exactly where you need to be, so take a deep breath and just relax and allow your emotions to flow.

(Woo hoo me on my journey LOL!)

ISSUES FACED BY CHILDREN AND YOUTH

You are the future and it is the responsibility of adults to protect you and ensure that you to get the best start in life. Unfortunately this is not always the case in many nations around the world, and including the UK. We have done some research, so take a moment to reflect on the worst situations that children and youth today are forced to face. It was very hard for my brother and I to believe that children and youth experience such horrific situations, but learning about them is a good way to start appreciating your health, happiness, family, friends, love, safety, support, access to education, opportunities and freedom you currently have. We ask you to think about how your life differs to theirs? What will you do to help children and youth across the globe to improve their quality of life? With the power of the internet and other technologies available to you combined with your **dream**s! You can become the change you want to see.

Trust your highest thought, your clearest words and your grandest feeling. Your highest thought is always the thought which makes your feel good. Your clearest words are the words which contain truth and honesty. Your grandest feeling is **LOVE**.

Around the world children and youth experience: Violence through Indoctrination, Poverty, Life as Refugees, Lack of Access to Education, Child Neglect, Child Labour, Child Prostitution, Internet Child Pornography, Trafficking and Slavery and Military Use of Children.

- How appreciative would these children and youth be to have your experience in exchange for theirs?

Here are some common issues that children and youth also experience: Single Parent Households, Drug/Alcohol Abuse, Growing up too fast, and Violence in Schools/Home etc, Materialism, Obesity, Education Disparity and Shifting Economy.

We encourage you to do some research yourself and speak to your friends, family, community centre and school to plant a seed to actively contribute to improving the lives of children and youth across the globe.

IT IS SIMPLY A MATTER OF CHOICE

Despite children and youth claiming that they lack confidence and that they never felt confident about anything in their entire life, when asked how confident they're about that statement many say very confident! LOL! Can you see where we are going with this? Yes or Yes?

The problem really isn't that they lack confidence, but they are confident about the wrong things. What you focus on, what you tell yourself and what you practice creates your reality.

Your task is to think of a problem and we want you to remember a time when you felt totally confident, go ahead and get in touch with your emotions.

- Do you remember a specific time? Yes or Yes?

Go back to that time **now**, go right back **now**. Hear what you heard, feel what you felt, see what you saw and really feel the feelings of being totally confident right **now**! Good job -it feels great doesn't it?

Now you **know** you can choose to feel confident whenever you desire, don't you? Yes or Yes?

(Me, *Tray-Séan, Johnnie Cass & Daniel Wagner*)

YOU HARNESS AN AMAZING ABILITY

Did you know that your brain encounters difficulty processing negatives? The good news is that by making a simple shift in the way you speak will produce profound changes in your life. Direct your attention away from what you do not desire and towards what you desire. FYI!... some children and youth spend too much time complaining about what they don't desire for example:

- "I don't want to fail my maths test"

Your brain will simply process it as "fail", because the more you think about NOT doing 'X', NOT wanting 'X'... The more you will think about 'X' and you will simply attract that very thing that you do not desire. Here is another example:

- "Don't laugh"

You first have to think of not <u>laughing</u>, then attempt to stop thinking about <u>laughing</u>. You may find that you can't help <u>laughing</u> (((**SMILE**))) LOL! Ha! Ha! Ha! This is because our brains can't think about NOT desiring something without first having to think about that very thing which you don't desire. What you think about, you simply bring about. We suggest that you focus on what you desire with deep heartfelt passion so much so that it feels "**AS IF YOU HAVE IT RIGHT NOW**"

Did you **know** that it is a scientific FACT *that our brain is unable to tell the difference between fantasy and reality because* the same neurological connections are stimulated? It is simple really all you have to do is say what you desire, **as if you have it now.** We encourage you to do so with absolute conviction and not like this "I will be wealthy". Instead say it like this "I am overwhelmed with gratitude now that i am wealthy" or "It is an amazing feeling wealthy" and always remember to (((SMILE))). **Whatever you do, don't laugh! Don't laugh (((SMILE))). We LOVE having FUN with that one LOL!**

NOW - are you ready to play full out? Yes or Yes?

We want you to stop and take a moment to visualise a specific time when you were totally motivated. Trust your unconscious... As you go back. Go right back to that time **NOW**. See what you saw, hear what you heard and really feel the feelings of being totally motivated... **Now** take a moment to fully experience your emotions.

WELL DONE!!! It feels great right? Yes or Yes?

When you visualise you'll materialise, we encourage you to practice your visualisation technique as often as possible. FYI! Some people find it useful to emulate a role model who has achieved your desired outcome. It will benefit you to **know** that we all process information using representational systems after receiving data through our five senses. These are sight, sound, touch, taste and smell plus self-talk. These allow us to translate the external world into an internal representation of reality and remember reality is different for each of us. There are four primary representational systems used to make these internal representations which are primarily: pictures, sounds, feelings and self-talk. Always be aware of what influences you in your daily environment: The music you listen to, the language you use, the environments you frequent in, self talk and the images just to name a few.

Now we want you to visualise a mixing bowl (you've done this one before - remember): add eggs, butter, flour, sugar and water. Mix it all together, and then place it into the oven... Would you be surprised to find you've baked a cake?

Consequently, if your life is filled with negativity for example: negative role models, negative language, get rich quick, disrespect, lack, struggle, negative images, negative experiences, negative music and negative people etc. The outcome is what presents in the individuals life. Its simple really if you do not control your mind, chances are someone else already is.

Are you ready to play? Yes or Yes?

We want you to list of your desired outcomes for the next 6mths - 1 year using the method below for each outcome:

- ✓ **BE CONCISE:** Clearly describe your desired outcome

- ✓ **BE REALISTIC:** Be mindful of your abilities, resources and unbounded potential surrounding you

- ✓ **FOR WHAT PURPOSE:** Make your motivation huge to fuel your desire, the **big**ger the '**WHY?**' the easier the '**HOW?**'

- ✓ **BE ECOLOGICAL:** Safe for you, safe for others and safe for the environment

- ✓ **ACT AS IF NOW:** Describe what you hear, feel, see, smell and self talk as if you are experiencing it **NOW**. Start your sentence like:

"I am", "I have" or "I see... feel, smell, touch" and so on.

- ✓ **WORK TOWARDS WHAT YOU WANT:** *I*nsert a deadline, positivity and productivity are absolutely paramount

- ✓ **END STEP:** How will you know when you have accomplished your desired outcome? For example: If your desired outcome is to graduate. Your end step may be when you hire your graduation gown... Remember there is no right or wrong answer, the end step is different for everyone.

NOW say: "I'm an action taker baby!", "I'm ready to take responsibility baby!", "I'm gorgeous", "I have a millionaire mind", "I'm a creator and ready to create the future I deserve" (((**SMILE**))).

(Me, Tray-Séan and Raymond Aaron)

CHOOSE TO BE HAPPY

Did you know that your mind, body and soul are seamlessly intertwined? Your physiology is connected to particular emotional states. Take a moment to remember a specific time when you were able to pick up on someone's emotional state just by observing their body language... you've done that right? Yes or Yes? Your emotional state determines your physiology and your physiology determines your emotional state. Happiness, joy and excitement are forms of emotional states.

- Did you k**now** that you can choose to experience the emotional state of happiness right **now**?

That's right - you can! There are many things you could do to make you feel happy for example play uplifting music, remember a **fun**ny/special memory, play with a family pet or watch others having **FUN** and you could simply change your physiology, yes that's right - a simply change is all it takes.

- Are you **willing** to play full out? Yes or Yes?

We would like you to do the following while seating or standing: Frown, look at the ground, droop your shoulders and hang your head. **NOW** take a deep breath.... **T**ry to think positive thoughts or say something positive... and find that you can't! **NOW** think negative thoughts or say something negative, and find that you are overwhelmed with sadness and negativity.

Be mindful of how you feel and preserve the positive learnings for yourself and future.

Now put a **HUGE (((SMILE)))** on your face, draw your shoulders back into a comfortable position, raise your head into an empowering position, and appreciate your environment by scanning your surroundings. **Now** take a deep breath... **now** try to think negative thoughts or say something negative, and find that you can't! **Now** think positive thoughts or say something positive, and find that you are overwhelmed with happiness, joy and positivity. Well done - you are the master of your mind right? Yes or Yes? Pay close attention to how you feel and preserve the positive learnings. **Now** go ahead and shake off any negative vibes and retain your positive emotional state - feels great right? Yes or Yes?

You harness the power to change your emotional state by a simply shift in your physiology, 24 hours a day, 7 days a week and 365 days a year. **Now** we want you to step out into some indefinite time in the future where in the past the old problem would have hindered you or held you back, notice how you are seeing things differently **now**! You are the master of your mind; all you need to do is put a **HUGE (((SMILE)))** on your face and change your physiology and you will instantly experience a significant positive shift in your emotional state. Are you ready to play? Yes or Yes?

We want you to think of the same problem or a different problem for each of the following exercises. You will need to carefully think about each question in each exercise. LOL! We encourage you to let go of logic for **now**:

Exercise 1: What is the problem?, What's the root cause of the issue?, How have you failed to resolve his?, How can you **overcome** the solution to your problem?, What would you like to transform?, When will you stop it from being a limitation?, How many ways do you k**now** you have solved this?, How are you changing and seeing things differently **NOW**? And how do you k**now**?

Exercise 2: What's the problem?, How do you k**now** it is a problem?, When did you decide that?, When don't you do it **NOW**? What are you deciding then?, How is it different from how you were?, How do you k**now** that **NOW**? And what other changes would you like to make?

YOUR DAILY TOOL KIT

If you experience a day filled with challenges, simply take out a pen and draw a (((**SMILEY FACE**))) on your index fingers. Any time you feel a little blue, it's time to unleash your (((**SMILEY FACE**))) LOL! How can you possibly take anything seriously when doing this? LOL! We encourage you to (((**SMILE**))) and greet strangers, far too many children and youth ignore each other or wear frowns when they are out and about; we have meet some of my closest friends today because we walked around (((**SMILING**))) and started conversations with total strangers.

You could be a friendly bear on the loose... LOL! LOL! Greeting your peers on a daily basis. LOL! We have every confidence that you will collect some funny stories to share with friends and family and make good friends too.

ASK – BELIEVE – RECIEVE

O-kay! The kind of life you **dream** of may appear out of reach for the moment; however we want you to take a moment to remember a week ago:

- What were you doing a week ago and how does your mind set differ **now**?

- What thoughts were you having?

- A week ago did you k**now** that you would be reading this book and making significant changes in your life?

- How many ways will your life improve with your new expanded awareness?

Yippee! Yippee! Yippee! You are making new connections and your reality is expanding because of the k**now**ledge you have gained. You are seeing things differently **now** and its feel great... right? Yes or Yes? (((**SMILE**))). All of your memories and associated incidents are stored in your unconscious mind. Your unconscious mind is the home of your empowerment, creativity, emotions, imagination and energy.

'DREAMS DO COME TRUE!'

We are sooooo excited about sharing this powerful process with you. **A**sk - **B**elieve - **R**eceive is the key to manifesting yours **dream**s:

1. **Ask** - you must k**now** what you desire... You must really k**now** what you desire. The universe can't deliver your desire without first

knowing what you desire to manifest into your life.

2. **Believe** - you have to maintain unwavering faith that what you desire will become **'yours'**. All uncertainties must be eliminated.

3. **Receive** - it is very important that you become an **action taker**. When opportunities present, you must **TAKE ACTION**! And do what presents; learn to be a generous giver and an excellent receiver **now**.

This is a proven technique; sports psychologists use this technique when training athletes. It is the difference that makes the difference, it determines if **YOU WIN** or lose. Remember your minds can't determine the difference between fantasy and reality.

- Are you ready to play? Yes or Yes?

FYI! Repetition is crucial, like anything in life practise makes perfect and relaxation is also a key factor. Below is a brief to prepare you for the visualisation process.

BRIEF

Relaxation: Relax your mind, body and soul so much so that you become at one with the visualization process. Experience the emotions and become fully aware of your movements, emotions etc taking place within your body.

Visualization: Make the mental image so realistic that you believe that you are actually doing it **now**. You must call upon all your senses and imagine what you can see, hear, feel, smell, taste and self-talk where applicable. You must believe as you will only achieve what you deem to be true.

Language: Become totally mindful of external and internal words that are associated to your desired outcome.

Now read each storyline until your become fimilar with it, then go ahead and close your eyes to experience the visualisation process. **It's time to play...**

Storyline 1: You are about to perform a serve in a badminton contest, the following components are associated: preparation, shuttlecock toss, impact of racket, ready position and shuttlecock flight then await opponents' reaction.

Now - take a deep breath and enhance this experience, by making the colour vibrant, turn up the sounds which surround you (self talk and what others are saying), notice the temperature.

See the shuttlecock in one hand and your racket in the other. Relax your shoulders and hands - feel the texture of the racket grip within the palm of your hands.

Feel the texture of the shuttlecock on your finger tips, as you prepare to launch the shuttlecock into the calm air. Notice how your arms do this effortlessly, you will become aware of the shift in your body weight as your elbows and knees bend to get into position. Notice how your body is rising as you prepare to strike the shuttlecock, notice the energy in your body as you connect with the shuttlecock. See the shuttlecock as it races through the air upon impact, **now** feel the relaxation within your body as you witness your opponent attempting to return the shuttlecock and realise that they do not and your body is filled with an overwhelming desire to express your excitement and pleasure.

Feels great right! - take a deep breath and just relax and preserve the positive learnings.

Storyline 2: CONCIOUSLY DESIGN YOUR DAY - take a moment to relax...

That's right just relax...

It feels right... To just relax **now**!

Deepen your relationship with yourself and the world around you right **now**. You will need to trust your unconscious and fully experience the process:

Take a deep breath and visualise tomorrow – Simply say the following:

- "I am taking this time to create my day, and I am infecting the universe with my desires"

Then go ahead and simply visualise each phase of the day from the time you awake until the point when you go to bed. Become fully aware of what you see, hear, feel, taste, smell and self talk. **NOW** go ahead relax, close your eyes and begin to visualize tomorrow...

NOW document all the details - in a moment not **NOW**. We want you to close your eyes and fully experience what you have documented. Be sure to end your visualisation process by taking a deep breath and then blow three huge breaths onto your desired outcome for tomorrow.

We truly believe that patients overcomes calamity. Tomorrow evening simply document what took place and then compare the two.

(((SMILE))) WELL DONE!! (((SMILE)))

(Me, Tray-Séan and Ewan Wong our yummy mummy's coach)

FORGIVE AND LET GO

This is not about blame or beating yourself up. This is an opportunity to forgive and let go. Did you **know** that blame, reasons and excuses will simply places you on the effect side of the equation and will leave you feeling disempowered. By taking responsibility you are ack**now**ledging your influence in the experiences, because even doing nothing is a choice you made – right? Taking responsibility will place you on the cause side of the equation and empower you to take control of your life. We both believe that things happen because of something we do or we don't do. Each and every choice you make has a set of positives and negatives associated to it. Taking responsibility is your first step towards your personal development because this will help you to rise up empowered.

By taking responsibility for your role in 'X' you will give yourself the ability to change 'X' and create your desired experience. Taking responsibility will destroy the 'victim mentality' and exchange it for a 'victorious mentality' (((**AWESOME**))). You are 'VICTORIOUS'...aren't you? Yes or Yes? Say it with us: 'I am victorious' and again 'I am victorious' and again 'I am victorious'. As soon as you are able to forgive and let go, the sooner you will be able to understand yourself, people and the world surrounding you.

Learn to respect other people's model of the world, being right is not always important – you can be right or you can be happy. The choice is always yours. Anyway most of your past negative experiences were never about you entirely. People simply act out how they are feeling inside. Holding on to regrets and bitterness will only stop you from moving forward in your life, so just **FORGIVE** yourself and the person/people in question for the past. Don't try to seek revenge by hurting them or breaking their pride, just forgive and let go now; then you will be ready to fly. (((SMILE))) you will feel better when you choose to **FORGIVE**.

Now! Preserve the positive learnings and accept the things which you can't change, commit to moving forward in your life. Don't worry if you hear the little voice in your head saying: "We could have...", "If only...." or "I should have..." it's normal, but **now** we want you to think about these questions:

- Are these thoughts making you feel better?

- Are these thoughts benefiting you?

- Are these thoughts empowering you?

- Are these thoughts moving your life towards your desired outcome(s)?

- What other thoughts will be more beneficial to you?

- What positive learnings can you preserve **now** to help you to **FORGIVE** and move towards having **FUN, DREAMING BIG** and making money doing what you **LOVE**?

Remember it does not matter what anyone else thinks of you, what matters most is what you think of yourself. The words that come from your mouth you are the first to hear. So speak words of positivity, because what you sow you shall weep. You have to heal your heart, you have to heal your body, you have to heal your mind and you have to heal your soul.

Now relax and take a deep breath... That's right! You are exactly where you need to be right **now**.

*Are you **ready to play**? Yes or Yes?*

For a moment we would like you to simply shift your focus to what you appreciate about each person in your life for example your mother, father, guardian, friend, family member, your grandparents etc. We believe that you will find this exercise therapeutic because it can help you to forgive and release negative energy (((**SMILE**))).

Now you are going to write a letter to each person who hurt you. No! No! No! LOL! Relax, relax... Don't worry... You will not need to mail the letter to them. When you have completed your letter read it until you preserve the positive learnings, then you can destroy it. Below is the layout you will need to use here goes... **now** we want you to insert the name of the person who you are writing the letter to:

Dear Friend I want you to k**now** _____ about my life. Friend I need you to hear _____. Friend in order to complete I need to say _____. Friend I am angry about _____. Friend I appreciate _____ about you. Friend I **forgive** you for ___

Once you have completed your letter write a response from your Friend saying: "Thank you for sharing this with me, please **forgive** me. I am sorry and I appreciate you."

Dear Mother I want you to k**now** _____ about my life. Mother I need you to hear _____. Mother in order to complete I need to say _____. Mother I am angry about _____. Mother I appreciate _____ about you. Mother I **forgive** you for ___

Once you have completed your letter write a response from your mother saying: "Thank you for sharing this with me, please **forgive** me. I am sorry and I appreciate you."

Dear Father I want you to k**now** _____ about my life. Father I need you to hear _____. Father in order to complete I need to say _____. Father I am angry about _____. Father I appreciate _____ about you. Father I **forgive** you for ___

Once you have completed your letter write a response from your father saying: "Thank you for sharing this with me, please **forgive** me. I am sorry and I appreciate you."

Now go ahead and read these letters until you have preserved the positive learnings. Once you have done so, destroy the letters. That was a terrible problem wasn't it, **now** as you step out to some indefinite time in the future where the old problem use to hold you back or cause you difficulty. Notice how you are seeing things differently **now** and it feels great right? Yes or Yes?

Go ahead and release past negative experiences... negative emotions... past insecurities and unwanted habitual actions... unproductive behaviours, unwanted negative thoughts and disempowering habits **now**. Well done!!

Now Replace them with a wealth of positivity... empowering thoughts... behaviours and habits, self talk. Go ahead and embrace your '**New Life**'.

It is common for each generation to blame the one before, because all of their frustrations come beating on your door. We can totally understand if you feel like a prisoner to all that your parent(s)/guardian(s) held so dear. You may also feel hostage to all their hopes and fears. Life is so precious and this is why we encourage you to forgive and let go **now**. At times you may feel that you're unable to gain agreement because others talk in defence. We are here to remind you that you always have a choice. Take time to think because you can be right or you can forgive, let go and be happy **now**. We encourage you to listen as well as you hear **now**. It's too late when we die, so just let go of the past and forgive. At times we quarrel between the present and past, but this simply sacrifices our future because it's the bitterness that lasts. As a direct message from our hearts to your heart, it's okay to let go of the past. Go ahead and just let go, its **now** time to simply **forgive and be (((FREE)))**.

(((CONGRATULATIONS))) – Embrace your new life filled with having **FUN**, **DREAMING BIG** and making money doing what you **LOVE** xxx

BULLYING

What is bullying?

Bullying is a form of aggressive behavior created by the use of force to affect others, especially when the behavior is habitual and involves an imbalance of power. There are many forms of bullying: cyber, emotional, financial, verbal and physical abuse.

Bullying ranges from single to gang bullying, when the bully may have one or more friends to assist in the act of bullying. Bullying can occur anywhere and by anyone: school, relationships, place of worship, family, friends, work, home, and neighborhoods etc.

Bullying is an act of repeated aggressive behavior in order to intentionally hurt another person, physically or mentally. Bullying is characterized by an individual behaving in a certain way to gain power over another person. Bullying behavior may involve name calling, verbal or written abuse, exclusion from activities, exclusion from social situations, physical abuse, or coercion. Bullies may behave this way to be perceived as popular or tough or to get attention. They may bully out of jealousy or be acting out because they themselves are bullied or have unresolved issues.

It is entirely common for children and youth to be totally unaware that they are being bullied if the signs are not obvious. We believe that bullying is the most important social issue that needs to be remedied and community cohesion needs to be encouraged, peer-to-peer support is a good way of developing strong relationships. Bullies fear exposure of their inadequacy and being held accountable for their behaviour. This makes sense when you remember that the purpose of bullying is to hide inadequacy.

Learn to deal with bullying:

- Learn to **LOVE** yourself and grow in confidence

- Seek support and advice straight away

- Speak to your parent(s)/guardian(s), teacher(s) or any responsible adult

- Know when bullying becomes dangerous

- Practice self defence techniques

- Avoid the environments where the bullies hang out and always travel with friends

- Practice what to say and do to get yourself out of a difficult situation and be assertive

- Have no fear of the bully and show kindness and **LOVE** towards them

- Control your anger and let the bully know that you are aware of their behaviour and demand that they stop!

- Keep a journal/diary, because this will help you to express your emotions

- Download "RED CARD IT!" and ask your school to book one of our "Kidz that **DREAM BIG!**" workshops

PLANT YOUR SEED FOR FINANCIAL EDUCATION

Do you find yourself:

- Constantly pointing your finger at others? Do you believe that the world is filled with of greedy people? The **LOVE** of money is the root to all evil? The government is to blame, the banks are irresponsible, my parents, my guardians and the economy etc, etc, etc?

If so!!... we are here to remind you that you could choose to spend a life time being a 'victim' or on the other hand you could in fact choose to spend a life time being 'victorious'?
Only you can choose....
If you point your finger at others, there are always three fingers pointing back at you and you are also giving your power away.

We are the Ben Salmi Duo and we are here to remind you that taking responsibility is the key to your success. Reclaim your power and exchange your adversities for empowerment:

- What can you do right **now** to help you take steps towards creating a life filled having **FUN, DREAMING BIG** and making **MONEY** doing what you **LOVE**?

- Do you know the difference between passive income and active income?

-

Allow us to explain... well at least what we know **LOL!:**

Active Income

E = **E**mployee. As an **E**mployee you work for someone else and they'll pay you an annual income. Your hours are set for you and your salary is usually paid monthly and there is usually a limit to what you can earn. As an employee, your boss controls you.

- Visualise how you could generate extra income?

- Visualise all areas of your lifestyle, what would and wouldn't be present?

SE = **S**elf-**E**mployed. As a **S**elf-**E**mployed individual you are the boss and you own your J.O.B for example: doctors, lawyers, actors and so on. You call the shots; you choose the hours you work. Your income can vary depending the hours you work; if you don't work you don't get paid. The longer you work the more you earn and the less you work the less you get paid.

- Visualise how you could generate extra income?

- Visualise all elements of your lifestyle, what would and wouldn't be present?

Passive Income

BO = **B**usiness **O**wner. As a **B**usiness **O**wner, you are the boss you use 1% of your time and 99% other peoples time, mind and energy to generate unlimited income. You make money while you sleep.

- Visualise how you could generate extra income?

- Visualise all elements of your lifestyle, what would and wouldn't be present?

I = **I**nvestor. As an **I**nvestor, you invest money for example into real estate, oil, gold, silver, platinum, palladium and so on. You make money while you sleep. Money works for you and generates you an abundance of wealth, not to mention time and financial freedom.

- Visualise how you could generate extra income?

- Visualise all elements of your lifestyle, what would and wouldn't be present?

Now that you have a better idea about passive income and active income will you choose to create a lifestyle which is fuelled by being an E, SE, BO or I? Have you ever thought about becoming an author, creating apps, setting up an online automated business, create a product or service?

We are here to tell you that your finance IQ will form the foundation for transforming YOU and help YOU to create a life filled with having **FUN, DREAMING BIG** and making **MONEY** doing what you **LOVE**.

More importantly it will help you to make educated judgements and effective decisions about the use and management of your money. If you want to become financially free you will need to mirror and match the mindset, habits, skill sets and traits of wealthy and successful people. For example what they do? What they do not do? And more importantly Why? People do not become wealthy because of luck. Did you **know** that there are strategies, formulas and systems which they live by?

Once you understand the purpose of **MONEY**, you will begin to see improvements in your finance health. LOL! FYI... Wishing to become wealthy will not make you wealthy, but if you choose to develop a burning desire to create wealth through a state of mind. Then the magic will begin to happen, because you will start to plan ways to generate wealth.

Did you k**now** that the rich convert earned income into either passive income/portfolio income and they compound their wealth to generate more and more wealth? It's true that they do this to generate cash flow to pay for their lifestyle. FYI... If you have negative beliefs surround money, exchange them for more empowering and positive ones **now**.

Are you ready to play full out? Yes or Yes? Awesome (((SMILE)))

Is it okay with your unconscious mind to make these changes NOW and have conscious awareness of it?

The thoughts you have relating to **money** will create your experience with **money**. It is very important for you to transmit positive thoughts about **money** today, to create wealth tomorrow. FYI!...The chances are your negative beliefs about **money** were learned from other people.

EXAMPLES OF NEGATIVE BELIEFS

- Money doesn't grow on trees
- Money is dirty and the root to all evil
- I am poor, but a good person
- Money is in short supply
- Money goes out faster than it comes in
- The cost of living is too expensive

- It's hard to hold onto money
- A penny saved is a penny earned
- It's better to save money for a rainy day
- Only greedy people have money
- Money only comes from hard work
- It's easier to spend than it is to save money
- Poor people can never become wealthy
- Money can't buy happiness
- I need money to make money
- I don't have good ideas to create wealth
- There is a limit to how much I can earn because I am only young
- I am not lucky, because good opportunities never come my way

Some of your negative beliefs relating to **money** are because of low self-esteem. Set an intention to get to the root cause of your disempowering beliefs **now**. Work on valuing 'yourself', because this will allow you to attract positive energy surrounding **money**. FYI! (((SMILE))) **money** will begin to flow to you more easily and effortlessly. FYI!... Like attracts like. You are a magnet so if you have thoughts of unworthiness, you will not attract wealth. Allow us to share some examples of low self-esteem beliefs:

- I do not deserve money, people like me can't become successful
- I'm not educated
- I can't create wealth
- I'm not liked by people
- It's selfish to think about myself, I like to help others instead
- I am not worthy
- Why try, I'll probably just fail anyway

- I'm not good enough to make money
- I'm no better than my parent(s)/guardian(s), brother(s), sister(s) etc - so I can't make more money than them
- I can't afford it
- I'm not good with money
- I'm such a loser
- If I'm successful, my friends and family will be jealous and stop liking me
- I'll never get a good job or become a business owner
- My parents are in debt and always will be in debt. So I guess I will be too
- I feel stuck, there aren't any opportunities or options for me
- Opportunities never come my way
- I'm scared that money will make me change into a bad person
- I hate wealthy people
- I'll never be able to make a lot of much money
- I'm too stupid to make money
- I'll inherit money someday
- It's difficult to create wealth if I'm poor at my school work
- My parents are poor, and I will be too
- I don't like change
- It's too difficult to make money
- Money can't make me buy me happiness, I'm happy without money
- I don't like giving money to charity, because I need it more than they do
- I'm not confident enough to ask for money
- I don't like being center of attention
- I'm a good giver, but not a good receiver
- I find it hard to spend money on myself

- I'm scared that I will fail
- I'm too young to become a millionaire
- I find it hard to value myself
- If I become a millionaire I'll have to pay higher taxes, so why bother?
- I can't control my life things just happen because everything is predetermined
- I don't like thinking about money
- If I become a millionaire, I will make friends who want me for my money and I don't want that

Here are some examples of negative values and beliefs that can prevent you from progressing in life:

- Without money, I'm worthless
- I don't have any control of my life, things just happen
- I don't like to **DREAM BIG**, I prefer to **dream** small incase I fail because my friends will laugh and think I'm silly
- I don't k**now** how to value or **LOVE** myself
- Money can't buy me happiness, more money will only bring more problems
- People like me can't create wealth
- Good things don't happen to me
- I'm always in the wrong place at the wrong time
- I have suffered all my life, so I guess my life will always be an experience of suffering
- I can't do what I **LOVE** because I can't get paid to do it
- I don't like responsibility, being responsible scares me

- Why waste time **dream**ing, when I can get a real job
- Life is meant to be a struggle, not a breeze that is how we learn
- Why would the universe/God help support like me
- I am a walking disaster, everything I touch goes wrong
- I'm not lucky
- I'm a realist, too many people waste time **dream**ing too much and thinking that they'll become a millionaire. I think they are crazy because **dreams** don't come true
- There's no such thing as miracles
- My parents are poor, their parents were poor so I will always be poor
- I don't like change, I feel safe the way I am
- It is too hard to try to create wealth
- I have a feeling that the future has nothing good for me
- I'll be okay, I always survive. I'll just take each day one step at a time
- There's no such thing as abundance, no body is perfect
- It's impossible to have it all - you can't be wealthy and happy, only poor people experience happiness.

We want you to think about the following question:

- What is money?

Did you k**now** that '**money**' is simply an exchange of value? Our yummy mummy gave us this example. In the past people would exchange gold, silver and even live stock. Money simply stores value by the meaning you we choose to give it. The amount of money you generate is a measure of your confidence, the amount of money you have is in line with the value which you believe yourself to be worth. Money is a measure of your positive thoughts and self-worth. The more you value yourself. The more confidence and self-worth you have, the more you are likely to attract and earn.

Here is another example, visualise two people doing exactly the same job. One person earns £7 per hour and another could earn ten times that amount just because of their confidence. Think about this for a moment a chicken salad sandwich can cost as little as £1 in one store and, £3 in another, £7 in another and even £25 in another. The exact same scenario can attract different results. Anything is possible, there really aren't any limits to how much you can earn as a business owner or investor. Don't just take our word for it, the next time you are out and about we challenge you to take a good look around and compare the differences in prices for a variety of products and services. We have been taught that it is not good to judge others. You may have heard people say:

- "Poor people are kind, nice and polite, but rich people are bad, dishonest and evil"

We have met many poor, middle class and extremely wealthy people and they have all been a mixture of kind-hearted, generous, evil, responsible, nice, rude and self-cantered individuals disregarding their financial background. Don't be disillusioned by assuming money makes people good or bad. There are good and evil people from all financial backgrounds, and you would be wrong to assume that the amount of wealth or material wealth that a person has is any indication of that person unless you ask them how they became wealthy an gained an insight to their personal journey. A person's wealth doesn't determine all of the individual's core values or beliefs whatsoever, so don't judge people prematurely and just know that there is always more to the story than what meet your eye.

If you have any of these negative values of beliefs or similar, we encourage you to exchange them for positive ones. Allow us to share some examples of beliefs which can empower you (((**SMILE**))):

EXAMPLES OF POSITIVE BELIEFS

- I am worthy
- I can do, be and have whatever I desire
- A sea of financial abundance will come to me
- Whatever I want and need will come to me
- I am exactly where I need to be, all will be well
- My financial IQ will constantly increase
- Creating wealth is a matter of choice
- I am surrounded with an abundance of wealth, health and happiness
- I am willing to do whatever it takes in order to become financially/time free
- Everything I desire is beckoning me right **now**
- It is **FUN** and effortless creating money
- I deserve to create wealth
- I will always find a way to manifest my **dream**s
- I'm the master of my mind and I'm always in control
- A good intentional will always bear good fruits
- I'm a generous giver and an excellent receiver
- Money works hard for me and makes me more and more money

- I earn enough passive income to create a life filled with having **fun**, **dreaming big** and making money doing what I **love**
- I'm financially free, I will work because I want to not because I have to
- I'm an excellent money manager and I always pay myself first
- I am a money magnet and I welcome money with open arms because money is an exchange of value and I value myself and others do too
- My personal story, skills and passion are unique and will create
- I **LOVE** money and money **love**s me
- I am my greatest asset
- I embrace wealth, health and happiness in abundance right **now**
- I k**now** that each and every penny I spend will be returned to me in abundance
- My part-time job is to create passive income streams that will allow me to effortlessly save, manage and invest my money
- I will attract the right people to help me to become wealthy and I have unwavering faith that I will achieve great results with the assistance of others
- I **LOVE** to receive money and I do it easily, joyfully and effortlessly
- I am able to raise seed capital for my **dream**s

Here's what we suggest you do from today: Feel good when spending money. If worry enters your mind replace it with an opposite thought. Focus on prosperity. Soak up good news, stories and programs because it will leave you feeling good about money. Talk about wealth, health, happiness, success and financial abundance everyday. Remember you are your greatest asset, resource and primary wealth. Align your intentions, values, beliefs and action with wealth, health, happiness and financial freedom. Select a positive role model who is financially healthy and learn from them. Read positive financial affirmations when you wake up and before you go to sleep. Visualise your abundant life several times a day. Create a list of resources that are currently available to you and another list of resources which you are seeking. In business act locally, but think globally and it is very important to reduce the time spent watching television, playing video game, talking on the phone and increase your time spent reading and studying to create your **dream**s. Make a note of all your ideas or create a vision board (we can help you to do this in a Kidz that dream big! Workshop). Appreciate the people in your life. **LOVE** yourself and learn to **forgive** yourself and others. Humble yourself so that you have no time to waste arguing or complaining. Listen to your heart, have **fun**, **dream big** and take action. Express gratitude and appreciation for every single thing you currently have in all areas of your life. Feel good and remain patient. Always k**now** that the universe has got your back and is on your side. Be a generous giver and an excellent receiver. Say "I am worthy and appreciate my wealth, health, abundance and happiness". Buy a gratitude pebble to remind you to appreciate life. Help others and do things to put a (((**SMILE**))) on their face. Draw a cheque for the amount of financial freedom you want to create, sign it and display it somewhere to be seen everyday. Form a small virtual (online) or physical group of people who aspire to attract wealth. Subscribe to professional wealth reaction newsletters and continue to immerse yourself in positivity. Learn from your experience and be the master of your mind.

Surround yourself with positive people and be as enthusiastic about their success as you are for yourself and more importantly feel the feelings of financial freedom right **now.**

To create wealth you will need to change the way you think about money because your thoughts cause your actions, because your thoughts and actions create results. Like us if you were raised in a poor or middle-class family, chances are you were not taught the **fun**damental tools needed to become financially free (we started learning with our yummy mummy a year ago). When our yummy mummy learned she taught us. *Are you ready to play fully out? Yes or Yes? Follow the instructions below:*

Be clear about the exact amount of money you want to create to become financial free. If you wrote down:
- "I earn £2000 passive income each month to get my parents out of debt"

This will simply reinforce your situation. So you must clearly declare an amount for example:

- "I'm totally overwhelmed emotions of joy and positivity **now** that I am financially free. I have £100,000 passive income credited to my account every month and my family and I life our lives having **fun**, **dreaming big** and making money doing what we **love**".

FYI!.. If you are thinking 'yeah right, WHATEVER!'. You will need to remember everything you have just learned in this book and then ask yourself these questions:

- How much is your life worth?

- Why do you believe that this amount is too outrageous?

- How do you intend to pay it forward, once you become financially and time free?

It is very important for you to allocate a date/deadline for your desired outcome. LOL! For example if you were expecting a present in the mail delivery we are sure that you would appreciate knowing an expected date of delivery...Yes or Yes? **Now**... we want you to write a detailed plan for generating wealth. We advise you to come up with at least 5 different methods to generate wealth. More importantly *TAKE ACTION* today... What can you do right *now*... Yes right '**now**' to kick start the domino effect, for example: find a coach, make a call, whether you are ready or not *JUST DO IT!* Last but not least you will need to read what you have written out aloud at least twice a day. It is extremely important that you believe, see and feel as if you are currently experiencing your **dream** in order to manifest it. Remember! Your brain does not **know** the difference between fantasy and reality. LOL!.. If you are thinking "It's impossible for me to experience my **dream,** if I don't have it". This is where your creative thinking, role play and **burning desire** will come in handy. When you truly **desire financial freedom** your **burning desire** will have no difficulty in convincing 'your brain' that you have acquired it.

Remember your objective is to **desire financial freedom** with all your might and to become so determined to have it that you are totally convinced that you will manifest it. There are so many amazing life stories about people who have done just as you are about to do and they successfully manifested their

financial and time freedom. Saturate your mind with a **burning desire** to attain **financial freedom** so much so that you can already see, feel and hear yourself immersed in your **dream**. **Now** ask yourself these questions:

- What would happen if you took **action**?

- What would happen if you do not **TAKE ACTION**?

- What would not happen if you do **TAKE ACTION**?

- What would not happen if you do not **TAKE ACTION**?

- How do you k**now**?

Are you ready to play full out? Yes or Yes?

Let's have some **FUN now**... Sing this in your best Mickey Mouse voice... Why do we have a feeling that you are saying "**NO** way"? LOL! Yes way (((**SMILE**))) Come on start singing. Stepping out of your comfort zone is the first step towards change.

"If you want to be somebody... And you want to go somewhere... You better wake up and pay attention... I'm ready to be somebody... I'm ready to go somewhere... I'm ready to wake up and pay attention...." WELL DONE

Now we want you to sing it again in any voice of your choice.

LOL! (((**EXCELLENT**))) Welcome to the new 'you'. **Now** let's get back to work... No matter how good you, your products or services may be... If no one k**now**s about you, your product(s) or service(s) nothing much will happen right!.

Multiple Oceans of Income:

- ✓ Active income is when you get paid for something you do for example: workshops, public speaking etc

- ✓ Passive income is when you earn money while you sleep for example: books, clothing, Apps or any form of business a system which operates without you

- ✓ Part-time income is when you only work a few hours for example: managing automated online business etc

STOP! Thinking about working for money and start thinking about how money can work for you and make you more and more money.... We are not going to buy into your reasons and excuses as to why you can't do 'X'- it's bad enough that you use to buy into it! Say it with us "I **LOVE** BEING A MONEY MAGNET" again... "I **LOVE** BEING A MONEY MAGNET" and again "I **LOVE** A MONEY MAGNET"... And again until you really feel it.

Come on... Stand up and jump up and down like you really mean it!

Don't worry about what others might think or say... FYI!... If you really want to become financially free you will have to be able to get over rejection, comments and fear. The only thing that really matters is what you think of yourself. If you want something go out and get it, don't allow anyone to tell you that you can't do, be or have 'X'? People only tell you that you can't do, be or have 'X' because they believe that they can't do, be or have 'X'. You have to take responsibility for creating your **dream**s and stop seeking external validation or acceptance from others who fail to follow their own **dream**s.

Now say it like you mean it "I **LOVE** BEING A MONEY MAGNET", each and every time you receive money, say thank you and then say "I **LOVE** BEING A MONEY MAGNET" no matter how small or large the amount. You must learn to become an excellent receiver and you will attract more.... Yippee! Yippee! Yippee! **Now** repeat after us and repeat 5 times with your eyes closed and 5 times with your eyes open do this for at least 28 days:

- ✓ I **LOVE** to think positively (point to your head)
- ✓ I **LOVE** to operate positively (shake your body baby)
- ✓ I **LOVE** to speak positively (point to your mouth)
- ✓ I **LOVE** to feel positively (place the palms of your hands on top of each other and then put them on your chest and feel the vibration as you speak)

We are the BEN SALMI DUO and we are your friends – ones you can trust. We believe in you, and it is about time that you start to believe in yourself. After all you are a creator, aren't you? Yes or Yes? You are creating your life right **now**.... This is not an opportunity to blame 'yourself' we just want to remind you that you are a *creator*. The good news is that you can **now** create your **dream**s (((SMILE))) are you ready to play? Yes or Yes?

We want you to visualise a room in your home that has an infinite amount of **money** inside... sounds good right! All you have to do in order to access that **money** is simply open the door, reach inside and take as much as you desire, as often as you choose, 24 hours a day, 7 days a week and 365 days a year (((**SMILE**))). **Now** ask yourself these questions:

- How many times a day would you take **money**?

- Visualise what you could do with that **money** right **now**?

FYI! We are here to tell you that you are the door to infinite cash flow and all you have to do is simply open the door to your **dream**s. Go ahead and simply reach inside yourself, because there are no limits. You harness the ability to unlock your **dream**s and create infinite cash flow... So what are you waiting for?

In order to create financial and time freedom, you will need to create a products or services. Remember there are no limits on what you can earn... sounds good right? Yes or Yes? Look at it this way, if you have a job you automatically have a limit to what you can earn because in most cases you are paid for your time. Slow down.... slow down... No we are not telling you to set up in business, well at least not straight away but we are telling you to explore your options. We must stress that it is never a good idea to jump into business blind, but we do encourage you to start small and grow **big**!... Keep your eyes wide open and your ears close to the ground, create a trusted network of support, develop a reliable and enthusiastic team and create a business that generates wealth and more importantly you have to be **willing** to work extremely hard short term to learn/create systems which will allow your business to **fun**ction without 'you' long term. Always remember to maintain the **FUN** factor. Yippee! Yippee! Yippee! **Now** that your energy levels are high, let's get back to work. We need you to understand that you can't mange time, because time waits for no one. Nevertheless you can learn to manage yourself more efficiently so answer these questions to help you gain clarity:

- What do you need to start doing more of with your time?

- What do you need to start doing less of with your time?

- What do you need to stop doing with your time?

- What do you need to start doing with your time?

It is very important to set aside 'ME TIME', friends' time and family time and time for what is importance to you.

Remember to surround yourself with positive people who you like and trust, people who believe in you, support you, inspire you and encourage you to be the best you can be.

Always remember the **big**ger your 'WHY' for manifesting your **dream**s the easier the 'How?' now we want you to think about these questions:

- Has your lack of money turned you into a fearful individual where money is concerned?

- Is your excuse for not giving to charity that you need the money more than they do?

- Do you scout for Freebies?

- Do you scout cheap 'X'?

- Do you forget to appreciate people who give you money?

Now we want you to visualise yourself financially and time free right **now**... Woo hoo it feels good right! Yes or Yes?

- What are you doing **now** that you are financially and time free?

Embrace your emotions of being able to purchase anything you desire, paying full price for 'X', travelling, rejecting discounts, donating generously to charities and even setting up your charity, sponsoring a **Love**d one or even a total stranger to pursue their **dream**s... it feels amazing right? Yes or Yes?

Money is energy and energy can't flow effortlessly if you continue to block it with negative values, beliefs or actions. We encourage you to make a conscious decision to allow positive energy around money to flow effortlessly in your life right here, right **now**. Ask yourself these questions:

- How would creating product(s) and/or service(s) improve your life?

Adopting a genuine generous persona will help you to create multiple pathways that will allow positive energy to flow effortlessly into your life. Saturate your mind with the belief that you are worthy and more importantly remind yourself that you deserve to have money flowing effortlessly in your life. Start valuing yourself, family and friends in your life and you will draw an abundance of positivity to you. Remember stepping out of your comfort zone is the first step towards personal development. Invest in 'you' for example purchasing more books, get a coach, save up to purchase seminar ticket(s), training and other empowerment tools. Whatever it may be for you, speak to your parent(s)/guardian(s) and **JUST DO IT!**

"We would like to commend you (((SMILE))) for reaching this point of our book. After all you made the choice to read this book right? Yes or Yes?"

Investing in 'you' will emit a really powerful message of your commitment towards creating your **dream**s. **Now** answer these questions:

- Do you value and **LOVE** 'yourself' and others?

- What will you do in order to value 'yourself' and others more?

Remember 'Money' is an exchange in value, therefore the more you value 'yourself' and others, the more you will create a president for others to value you too and consequently you will attract more money. A lack of value for 'yourself' will simply devalue you, your products or services. When you are not valuing yourself and others enough, you attract a lack of value. If for any reason you are also giving away too much for free, good at giving and not good at receiving, forgetting to treat yourself, letting people off even when you feel offended or simply not valuing yourself. It's time to get tough and set boundaries **now**! Do you agree? If for any reason you find it challenging to get tough around setting boundaries we suggest that you speak to a **love**d one or find a mentor. Think long and hard about your self-worth, because as soon as you value yourself more people will automatically perceive that you deserve to be valued and more importantly you are worthy for that or better aren't you? Yes or Yes? Now answer this question:

- Are you ready to begin your adventure to create financial freedom?

Focus upon improving 'yourself' and maintain unwavering faith that in time you will develop your own unique mastery followed by your own artistry of attracting positive energy in abundance and effortlessly. Let it be your prerogative to persistently seek constructive feedback from friends and family because this will help you to learn where you need to continue to make positive changes.

Now it's time to reclaim your power and totally commit to improving your financial health; we have every confidence that you will be amazed at the results once you fully commit to the process. In order to create wealth you will need to grow to become action orientated, fully charged and commit to making things happen – you can do that right? Yes or Yes? It's common for people to fall due to 'not **taking action**'; they then complain that they're not getting results. We encourage you to start getting busy **now**; only 'you' can choose to make things happen! After all you are a creator - right? Yes or Yes?

- What will you choose to create next?

FYI!.. There is a wealth of raw materials to support each and every one of your **dream**... It does not matter what you do, we only encourage you to do something you are passionate about. Don't worry too much because you will learn along the way and just make sure that **you** make each and every day count and more importantly have **fun**. FYI if it doesn't grow you it is not worthwhile your time. We are talking about partaking in negative conversations, watching television endlessly, texting, gossiping etc. We are also talking about the reasons and excuses for not taking action... whatever it may be for you STOP! STOP! STOP! Right **now**... Just go ahead a dump those old disempowering habitual actions and exchange them for new empowering ones (((SMILE))). Being a proactive master of your mind will change who you are and will carry you a long way over time! More importantly install the tenacity to complete each and every project you start, because you will gain valuable lessons in every experience. Can you visualise going to the fridge, opening a pot of yogurt eating half and then placing it back into the fridge. Then taking out another and another and another and doing exactly the same thing? Doing this will not benefit you, in fat if your house rules are anything like ours you would simply land yourself in **big** trouble LOL! Jokes aside it would not benefit you at all to do such a thing.

Our mission is to help you to recognise that **you are a creator** and to remind you to pursue your **dream**s no matter what. Those **dream**s that have you '**leaping out of bed**' each morning, go ahead and saturate yourself in your **dream**s right **now**. (((SMILE))) So much so that when you talk to others about your '**DREAM**S' your entire physiology illuminates. (((SMILE))) You have something special to contribute to our world and you have a burning desire to acquire k**now**ledge to enhance your life so the question we want to ask you **now** is:

- What seeds will you plant today for a brighter tomorrow?

-

DREAMS DO COME TRUE

We believe that having **FUN**, **DREAM**I**NG BIG** and making **MONEY** doing what you **LOVE** is the key to success. As a family we always encourage each other to be the best we can be. We would like to share this list of YOUNG MILLIONAIRES! With you, who knows... if you use your imagination maybe you will be added to this list one day? Sounds good right? Yes or Yes?

YOUNG MILLIONAIRES LIST

- Adam Hildreth was 14 went into business and at 19 he was one of the richest teens in the UK.

- Ashley Qualls was 17 when she became millionaire selling MySpace layouts to teenage girls.

- Cameron Johnson was 12 when first earned $1,000,000.

- Chris Phillips had made nearly £2 million as a teenager operating his own web company.

- Fraser Doherty 14 started making and selling homemade jam and became a millionaire.

- James Murray Wells online retailer selling eyeglasses and became a millionaire.

We challenge you to do some research to find out more about them and others

WE BELIEVE IN YOU!

We believe you can fly, we believe you can touch the sky. Have **FUN**, **DREAM BIG** and make **MONEY** doing what you **LOVE**.

Visualise yourself living your **DREAM**S. **LOVE** life, **LOVE** people and live your life with passion and purpose. Be a positive role model to your peers and always listen to your heart. Your life will be amazing, all you have to do is plant the seed today for a brighter future tomorrow (((**SMILE**))).

Remember you don't grow the **dream**, your **dream**s grow you:

- Expect support

- Expect a miracle

- Expect and cheque or even several cheques

- Expect expanded awareness and progress

- Expect financial and time freedom

Believe in yourself now and just know that all will be well (((SMILE)))

(Jeff Vacek, me and Ken Preuss)

MAKE MONEY DOING WHAT YOU LOVE

Some things are guaranteed in life and one of them is *CHANGE.* Our environment has changed, our awareness has changed, our lives have changed, our desire has changed and our opportunities have changed: Online shopping, Technological advancements, Medical advancements, Social media and Global recession.

Open your eyes and you will see new concepts. Some of your old concepts will no longer serve you well so we encourage you to dispose of them **now**.

You may be thinking... "What does all this have to do with 'ME'?" **Now** is your unique opportunity to have **FUN**, **DREAM BIG** and make money doing what you **LOVE**. It's **now** possible to successfully pursue your aspirations thanks to an awesome resource known as the internet (it is an extremely powerful tool). There are so many stories about children and youth just like you, who have become millionaires from the comfort of their bedrooms, through their online businesses.

Yippee! Yippee! Yippee! We **LOVE** the word (((FREE))), (((FREE))), (((FREE))) sounds good – right? Yes or Yes? There are sooooooooooooooo many (((FREE))) resources just waiting for you on the internet:

- So what's stopping you from taking action?

- What value can you add to other people's lives?

- What difference would you **LOVE** to make?

- What do you **LOVE** doing?

- What are you good at?

- Visualise your team required to support the delivery of your product or service?

- How many ways can you have **FUN, DREAM BIG** and make money doing what you **LOVE**?

OMG! Yippee! Yippee! Yippee! This is such an exciting time to be alive, because the internet has changed everything; it allows you to connect with likeminded people across the globe from the comfort of your home.

E-commerce technology allows you to sell products and services across the globe. Did you know that you can setup social network profiles for free? Did you also know that you can source and delivery products or services easily/cheaply? You can have thousands of followers worldwide and get them all excited about your products and services for free, you can video call them all free, and you can write them electronically for free too (((**SMILE**))):

- We trust that you are you getting the idea?

Let us put it this way... Your old mindset created your current experiences and reality. The Ben Salmi Due are here to tell you that it is time to let to convert your adversities into empowerment by preserving the positive learnings from your past. Go on embrace the present and allow yourself to have **FUN, DREAM BIG** and make money doing what you **LOVE – go on ask yourself this**:

- What are you passionate about?

- What problems have you experienced or heard of?

- What solutions can you come up with to solve these problems?

- What products or services can you market via the internet to generate a huge ROI (return on investment)?

- Do you **know** how to obtain free/cheap domain name and hosting for at least 1 year? (if no, do some research)

- Are you excited? You should be! (((**SMILE**)))

(Tray-Séan holding his dream board)

WHAT THE EXPERTS SAY

1) Start something while you are young. You have less responsibilities and if it does not work out first time you will learn from it and be better the next time you start something.

2) Make sure that there is a strong demand for your product or service, before you start.

3) Find out who you will be competing with and figure out a strategy.

4) Make your work a **FUN** place. This helps to motivate your team and also yourself!

Malcolm Graham
CEO Lime Tree Online
02075336634
07912106885
www.limetreeonline.com
mg@limetreeonline.com

Feng Shui to help support children, especially those having a hard time at school.

by Master Sarah McAllister - a Feng Shui consultant and horoscope specialist with over 14 years experience.

A bullied kid will be suffering from fear and lack of confidence, so you really need to make sure their home environment is supportive.

Bedroom Tips to Create a Supportive Space

If possible give children separate beds, not bunk beds as they tend to feel oppressed by either the ceiling or the top bunk. Wooden bedframes are preferable to metal ones and make sure the beds have good solid headboards. Place beds so there is a nice solid wall behind the headboard - this helps the child feel more secure. Their back is literally covered.

Study Tips

Place desks so that the chair has its back to a solid wall and child is overlooking the room or preferably looking out a window to the side too. Do not place desk against the bedroom wall to save on space, otherwise the kid is facing a brick wall, both actually and metaphorically speaking! Allow kids to study at kitchen table, as sometimes they just need to have people nearby in order to concentrate.

Respect their gut instincts

Little people have very good instincts and will know what colour they want in their room or where they want to sit to study, respect this always.

Put their artwork and pictures of friends on the bedroom wall

It sounds obvious, but some parents overlook this and leave a child's room bare and austere. Kids (and adults) **LOVE** to see images of their friends and also symbols of their success around them. Ideally place these pictures above eye level, as looking upwards activates vision and aspiration, whereas looking downwards concentrates us in the past.

Keep Electrosmog at a minimum in their bedroom

Electrical alarm clocks, cordless phones, mobile phones, computers - all must be either switched off or kept out of the bedroom so that the energy can settle during the night time and not interfere with the delicate bioelectrical field of your child which is still developing.

Use Natural Paints & Organic Materials if possible

Indoor air can be more polluted than outdoor air, so a good air filter is recommended, and use of natural paints. Chemical paints and artificial fabrics can create allergies in your child. The last thing they need is a skin condition or unsightly reactions due to allergies when they are already feeling vulnerable at school.

Use Chinese Horoscope Wisdom to help your child

Ask us to 'open the horoscope' of your child - we can decipher whether there is the presence of unhelpful authority (bullying) in the chart and advise colours to wear (as underwear if they have to wear a uniform), little pictures or totem animals to carry with them to support their chi, what foods are helpful to them and which directions within the house are best to occupy. *We had one mother from Croydon concerned with the amount of tickings off her son was getting at school, and my students and I went round to do a case study, moved his bed to a more empowering position and lo and almost overnight there was no more trouble. I also helped a kiddie in Holland Park to sleep through the night (previously waking up at 4am and bouncing into the parents room!) just by moving her bed to a more supportive area of the room and aligning it to 'quiet' energy as opposed to 'active' energy.*

Another young boy with Attention Deficit Disorder was immediately helped by moving the position of his bed and performing a space clearing - the father was initially sceptical, but developed a respect for what I had done based on the results he had witnessed.

This type of refined, intricate and powerful classical Feng Shui is not a self-help subject - the above pointers are useful basics, but do not substitute a professional Feng Shui consultation and horoscope analysis. For further information please visit www.myfengshuifriend.com or call 0844 848 4099 or email info@fengshuiagency.com.

Readers of this book can quote BENSALMI to receive a 15% discount until August 2012

CHILDREN AND YOUTH I URGE YOU TO DREAM BIG

Having **dream**s can make you feel happy. The more important that your **dream**s are to you, the more you will want to hold on to it!!

I want you to take a moment to think about what you would do if you weren't afraid to have **FUN**, **DREAM BIG** and make **money** doing what you **LOVE**? That's right... Just go ahead and allow yourself to feel your deepest and wildest **dream**s deep within your heart. After all we all have **dream**s... right? Yes or Yes? Fear simply holds you back. Remember you are a *creator*, when you choose to move beyond your fears you can begin to feel free.

If you do not change you can become extinct, lets face it... change is always happening.

Each and every day visualise your **dream**s as often as possible... imagine yourself enjoying your **dream**s because it can leads you to it. Movement in a new direction can help you achieve your **dream**s... so don't worry too much about being different to your peers. Difference is also good, so follow your own **dream**s and remain true to yourself.

The quicker you let go of peer pressure and your old negative values and beliefs, the sooner you can find new positive values and beliefs that will serve you well. When your values and beliefs change so will your life.

It will serve you best to pursue your **dream**s instead of simply living your life in default mode following your peers etc. We both know that holding onto old negative values and beliefs will not lead you to new positive results. When you realise that you can achieve your **dream**s, your life will begin to transform if you choose to. Acknowledging small change early can help you to adept to **big**ger changes that are to come, simply allow your **dream**s to flow and then you can begin your dance with the universe.

Sabrina Ben Salmi BSc

Email: info@sabrinabensalmi.com Website: www.sabrinabensalmi.com

WORDS FROM THE HEART OF A GRANDMOTHER

Parents: You have to help our children and youth, because they are tomorrow's leaders. If your child has a **dream,** you must help them to nurture that seed for it to grow. Without TLC that seed can not grow and your Childs' **dream** will surely die. It is not about pushing or pressuring your child. Ask your child how you can be of assistance and best support them to grow their **dream**? If you notice that your child is reaching out for support with a desire to be creative. Encourage them in each and every way, but always remember that it is your child's **dream** not yours. Also too much pressure could disrupt their creative process. Take one step at a time and enjoy the experience with them. Simply embrace this priceless experience together and give them a little independence as this will help them to learn valuable life lessons along the way.

Children and Youth: If you have a **dream** do not let anyone take your **dream** away from you because that **dream** is yours and it was created by you and no one but you has the ability to breath life into your **dream**. Always believe in yourself and your **dream**s 100%. There is no such thing as too young; even if you are 5 years old give it your all. In the end at least you will know that you have at least tried your best.

Mary Paul

Email: marypaulinterior@yahoo.co.uk
Website: www.wowthankyou.com/marypaulcreations

CONNECTING THE DOTS & GETTING STATRTED

Create a table that looks like the one below using the following headings: Name, E-mail, Contact Number and Possible Support.

Name	E-mail	Contact Number	Possible Support
Nancy	nancy@hotmail.com	07510342008	Brainstorm team member
Tom	tom@wow.co.uk	07823512098	Brainstorm team member
Live Unltd	info@liveunltd.com	02075662000	Grant, mentoring etc
May	may@ya.co.uk	07795551232	Website & business card designs
Mum/ Dad	Mum&dad@home.com	07777251982	Practical and moral support

Once you have completed this promise to make contact with each individual listed and talk to them about your **dream**s. Clearly explain the possible support which they can give you and more importantly offer to assist them in some way.

BOOKS:

- How To Be A Student Entrepreneur by Junior Ogunyemi
- Rich Dad, Poor Dad for Teens by Robert Kiyosaki
- Conversations with God for teens By Neale Donald Walsch
- The Little Soul and The Sun by Neale Donald Walsch
- The Little Soul and The Earth by Neale Donald Walsch
- Raising CEO Kids by Dr Jerry Cook & Sarah Cook
- Who moved my cheese by Dr Spencer Johnson
- Think and Grow Rich by Napoleon Hill
- Key Person of Influence by Daniel Precisely
- The Secret by Rhonda Byrne
- The Hidden Messages in Water by Dr Masaru Emoto
- I THINK I AM by Louise L. Hay
- The Story of The Ethical Elephants by Catherine Warrington

DVDs:

- The Secret
- What The Bleep Do You Know?
- Thrive

OTHER RESOURCES:

- Building Brands: www.buildingbrands.com
- Marketing File: www.marketingfile.com
- Fiverr: www.fiverr.com

- Survey Monkey: www.surveymonkey.com
- Cision PR & Communications: www.cision.com
- British Library Business & IP Centre: www.bl.uk/bipc
- CEO Email Addresses: www.ceoemail.com
- Clearlyso: www.clearlyso.com
- Grant Finder: www.grantfinder.co.uk
- BERR: www.berrgov.uk
- Unity Node: www.unitynode.org
- Talking IT Global: www.tigweb.org
- NBAN: www.nban.co.uk
- HMRC national advice service: www.hmrc.gov.uk
- Money Facts: www.moneyfacts.co.uk
- Apprenticeships: www.apprenticeships.org.uk
- 365 Tickets: www.365tickets.com
- Merlin Annual Pass: www.merlinannualpass.com
- Family Railcard: www.familyandriends-railcrad.co.uk
- East London Business Alliance: www.elba-1.org.uk
- British Dyslexia Association: www.bdadyslexiaorg.uk
- Mansa the high IQ society: www.mensa.org.uk
- Unltd: www.unltd.org.uk
- Khan Academy: www.khanacademy.org
- Starfall: www.starfall.com
- **Lashai Ben Salmi: www.lashaibensalmi.com & www.lashaibensalmi.co.uk info@kidzthatdreambig.com**
- Book Trust: www.booktrust.org.uk
- Peter Jones: www.peterjones.tv
- Urban Unlimited: www.uunetwork.co.uk

- Bright Ideas: www.brightideastrust.com
- Livity: www.livity.co.uk
- So You Wanna Be In TV?: www.soyouwannabeintv.com
- Shell Livewire: www.shell-livewire.org
- Bold Achievers Club: www.boldachieversclub.com
- School For Startups: www.schoolforstartups.co.uk
- Young Entreprenur Society: www.youngentrepreneursociety.org.uk
- UK Intellectual Property Office: www.patent.gov.uk
- Waterlow Legal: www.chambersdirectory.co.uk
- Get British Business Online: www.gbbo.co.uk
- Business In The Community: www.bitc.org.uk
- The Prince's Trust: www.princes-trust.org.uk
- Your Hidden Potential: www.yourhiddenpotential.co.uk
- Raising CEO Kids: www.raisingceokids.com
- The Secret: www.thesecret.tv

Sponsors **we appreciate all of the advice, support, opportunities and so much more that we get from you all:**

- Dawn Gibbins: www.dawngibbins.com
- Lime Tree: www.limetreeonline.com
- Andrew Sage: www.asae.co.uk.com
- Froggo Marketing: www.froggomarketing.co.uk
- Robert G. Allen: www.robertgallen.com
- Live Unltd: www.liveunltd.com

- Sabrina Ben Salmi (Mother): www.sabrinabensalmi.co.uk
- Mary Paul (Grandmother): www.wowthankyou.com/marypaulscreations
- Junior Ogunyemi: www.linkedin.com/pub/junior-ogunyemi/1a/123/305
- Alex Browning: www.alexbrowning.tv
- ClearlySo: www.clearlyso.com

Trust yourself, as you **know** more than you think you do. Simply inhale inspiration and exhale action. **Go** ahead and do what you **know** you ought to do. The answer you have always been waiting for is yes you can, do, be and have whatever your heart desires.

It is an absolute honour to welcome you to the family. What are you going to do to celebrate your achievements?

((((CONGRATULATIONS))))

Here's to your wealth, health and happiness xxx

ABOUT THE AUTHORS

LASHAI BEN SALMI is 11 years old and the eldest of four, author, enlightened social entrepreneur and founder of: My Journey - "Giving youth several reasons to (((SMILE)))", Mega Lash-Lash Competitions, Co-creator of Put The RED CARD up to bullying & Fashion Lash-Lash.

Lashai went from being a victim of bullying with a host of associated adversities to becoming passionate about inspiring children and youth to convert their adversities into motivation so that they can have *FUN*, *DREAM BIG* and make money doing what they *LOVE* so that they may rise up empowered. Lashai is filled with a **dream** and a burning desire to enrich the lives of children and youth in her local community and across the globe. Lashai chose to convert her adversities into empowerment in the hope of inspiring her siblings and youth just like you to do the same or better.

Lashai has been featured in online articles: CEO Kids, Your Hidden Potential, ClearlySo and news papers: Voice, Ilford Recorder to name a few. Lashai has been interviewed by Lewis Johnson (brother of Boris Johnson Mayor of London), Pitched at ClearlySo conference, attended prestigious events like: Millionaire Bootcamp for Women, T Harv Eker: Millionaire Mind intensive, Robert G. Allen: Multiple Streams of Millions, TEDx Salford to name a few. Lashai has also won three awards: Live Unltd , Young Citizens Award and Black Youth Achievers Award (Lashai is also a **BYA Ambassador**). Lashai has teamed up with junior brother Tray-Séan Ben Salmi to co-create their first mobile App: Put the RED CARD up to bullying – which aims to reduce bullying and encourage community cohesion through skill swapping. Lashai has huge **dream**s and is planting seeds to enable her to have **FUN**, **DREAM BIG** and make money doing what she **LOVES**. In addition Lashai **dream**s of a future rich in abundance of financial and time freedom.

Lashai **LOVE**s life, youth social entrepreneurship, art, science, and mathematics. Lashai is also fascinated by the intricacies of the mind, our surrounding environment, being fully alive and dancing with the universe.

Lashai expresses absolute gratitude for being fortunate to have access to a very exclusive network of individuals, events and experiences.

TRAY-SÉAN BEN SALMI is 7 years old and the second eldest of four, author, enlightened social entrepreneur and founder of: Our Journey, Mega Shuby Competitions & Fashion Shuby.

Our Journey - "Giving children several reasons to (((SMILE)))"

Tray-Séan went from being a victim of bullying with a host of associated adversities to becoming passionate about inspiring children to convert their adversities into motivation so that they can have **FUN**, **DREAM BIG**, make money doing what they **LOVE** so that they may rise up empowered. Tray-Séan teamed up with his senior sister Lashai Ben Salmi is filled with a **dream** and a burning desire to enrich the lives of children & youth across the globe. They chose to convert their adversities into empowerment in the hope of inspiring their siblings, children and youth just like you to do the same.

*Tray-Séan **Ben Salmi*** is 7 years old and the second eldest of four, author, enlightened social entrepreneur and founder of: Our Journey - "Giving children several reasons to (((**SMILE**)))", Mega Shuby Competitions, Co-creator of Put The RED CARD up to bullying & Fashion Shuby.

Tray-Séan is a fairly shy yet dapper young man who has huge **dream**s. Since teaming up with his senior sister Lashai – Tray-Séan has gone from being shy to becoming passionate about inspiring children and youth to convert their adversities into motivation so that they can have **FUN**, *DREAM BIG* and make money doing what they *LOVE* so that they may rise up empowered. Tray-Séan is filled with a **dream** and a burning desire to enrich the lives of children and youth in his local community and across the globe. Tray-Séan chose to convert his adversities into empowerment in the hope of inspiring her siblings and youth just like you to do the same or better.

Tray-Séan has been featured in online articles: CEO Kids and news papers: Voice, Ilford Recorder to name a few. Tray-Séan has attended prestigious events like: T Harv Eker: Millionaire Mind intensive, British Library private receptions and TEDx Salford to name a few. In addition Tray-Séan **dream**s of a future in abundance of health, wealth, financial and time freedom.

Tray-Séan **LOVE**s life, child social entrepreneurship, mathematics, football and science. Like Lashai Tray-Séan is also fascinated by the intricacies of the mind, our surrounding environment, being fully alive and dancing with the universe.

Tray-Séan expresses absolute gratitude for being fortunate to have access to a very exclusive network of individuals, events and experiences.

We would both like to thank you for taking your time to read our book
xxx Ask your school and community centre to book a "Kidz that DREAM BIG" workshop xxx

Email Us:

Info@kidzthatdreambig.com

Info@lashaibensalmi.com

Info@puttheredcarduptobullying.com